FRAGILE DEMON

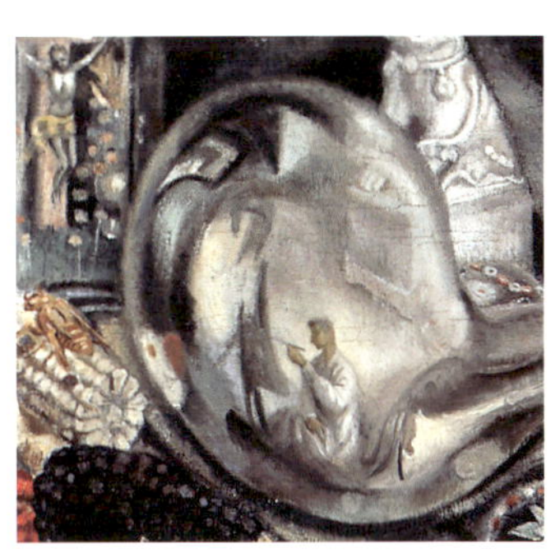

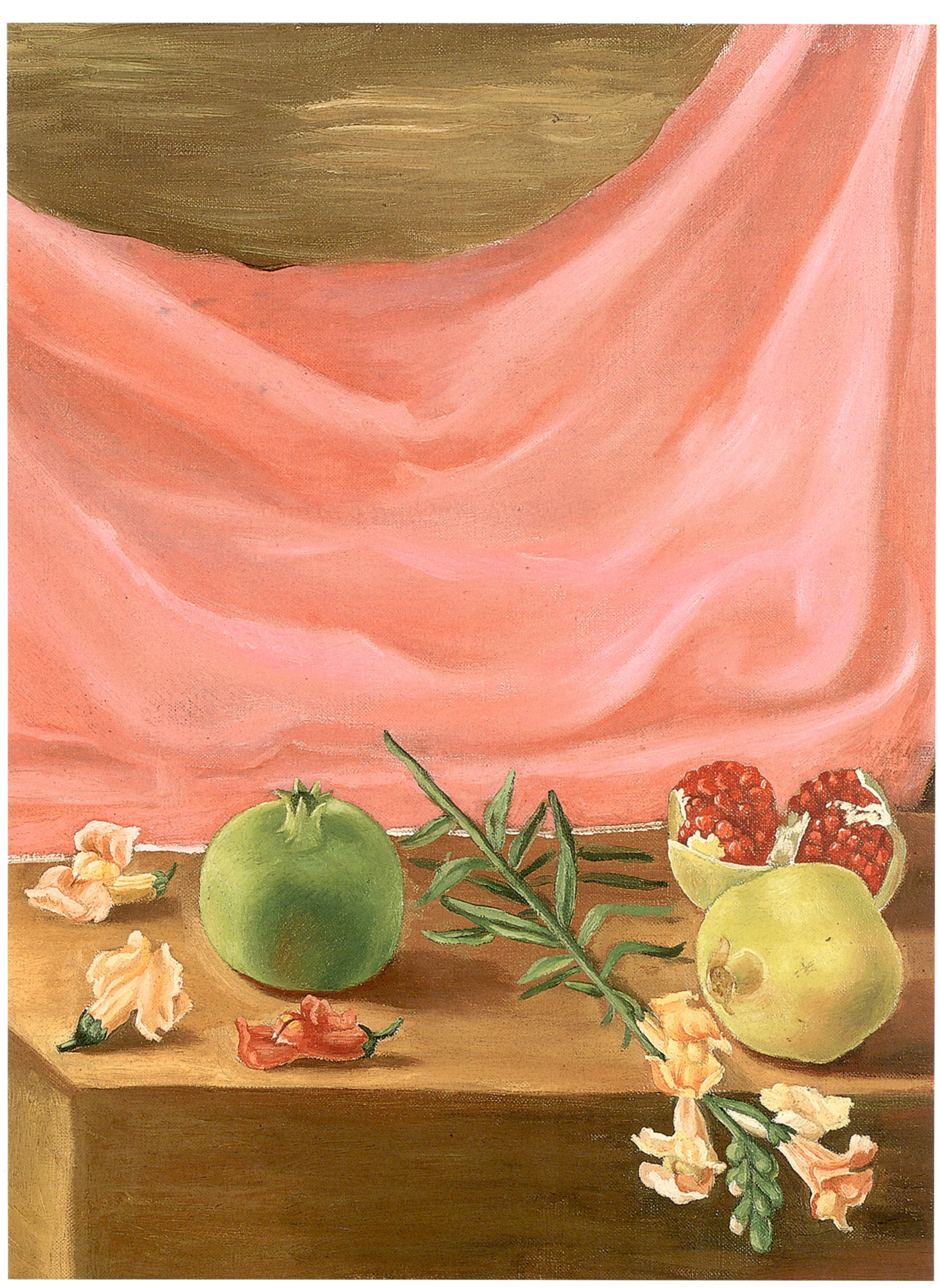

FRAGILE DEMON

Juan Soriano in Mexico, 1935 to 1950

Edward J. Sullivan

With texts by Octavio Paz and Carlos Fuentes

PHILADELPHIA MUSEUM OF ART

in association with

YALE UNIVERSITY PRESS

NEW HAVEN AND LONDON

This *Bulletin* was published on the occasion of the exhibition *Fragile Demon: Juan Soriano in Mexico, 1935 to 1950*, at the Philadelphia Museum of Art, February 16 to May 11, 2008.

The exhibition was made possible by Telcel, Fundación José Cuervo, and a generous anonymous donor. The catalogue was supported by The Andrew W. Mellon Fund for Scholarly Publications.

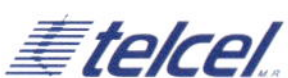

Telcel is honored and delighted to support *Fragile Demon: Juan Soriano in Mexico, 1935 to 1950.*

Experience great expressions of art with Telcel.

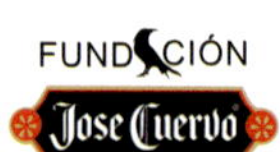

Fundación José Cuervo is delighted to encourage cultural exchanges between Mexico and the United States, and is especially pleased to bring the work of Juan Soriano to new audiences with this monographic exhibition dedicated to the artist.

Spring 2008, Volume 94, Numbers 395–96

Front cover: Lola Alvarez Bravo (Mexican, 1907–1993). *Portrait of Juan Soriano* (detail; see p. 8 for full image), c. 1937–38. Fundación Juan Soriano y Marek Keller A.C., Mexico City. Courtesy Center for Creative Photography, University of Arizona, © 1995 The University of Arizona Foundation

Back cover: Juan Soriano (Mexican, 1920–2006). *Child with Bird*, 1941 (fig. 19)

Half-title page: Juan Soriano, *Still Life with Self-Portrait* (detail), 1949 (fig. 16)

Frontispiece: Juan Soriano, *Still Life* (detail), 1942 (fig. 12)

Published by the Philadelphia Museum of Art
in association with
Yale University Press, New Haven and London
www.yalebooks.com

Edited by Sherry Babbitt
Production by Richard Bonk
Designed by Dean Bornstein
Printed and bound in Canada by Transcontinental Litho Acme, Montreal

Photography Credits:
Fundación Juan Soriano y Marek Keller A.C., Mexico City: frontispiece; pp. 8, 11, 12; figs. 2–9, 11, 14–18, 21–27, 29–34, 41, 42. Gilcrease Museum, Tulsa, Oklahoma (photograph © Javier Hinojosa): fig. 38. Eric Mitchell: fig. 28. Museo Andrés Blaisten, Mexico City (photographs © Javier Hinojosa): figs. 20, 40. Museo Soumaya, Mexico City (photograph © Javier Hinojosa): fig. 1. The Museum of Modern Art, New York: Digital image © The Museum of Modern Art / Licensed by SCALA / Art Resource, NY: fig. 19. Andrea Nuñez: fig. 37. Graydon Wood: figs. 10, 12, 13, 35, 36

ISBN 978-0-300-13688-3

READER'S NOTE
All works are by Juan Soriano unless noted otherwise. Works included in the exhibition are indicated with an asterisk (*) before the figure number.

Contents

Foreword

The commitment of the Philadelphia Museum of Art and successive generations of its trustees, donors, directors, and curators to the splendid and varied arts of Mexico began at the turn of the twentieth century, when the young Museum received a notable gift of colonial Mexican paintings from Dr. Robert H. Lamborn in 1903. The decorative arts for which Mexico is justly renowned arrived shortly thereafter, when the enterprising curator Edwin AtLee Barber added a splendid group of Talavera ceramics to his extraordinary range of purchases (which included Pennsylvania German redware and Tiffany glass) for the Museum collections. The gift in 1950 from the celebrated collectors Louise and Walter Arensberg, not only of their superb early modern holdings but also of their pre-Columbian art, brought important examples of Aztec sculpture.

After the Museum took possession of its monumental new building on Fairmount in 1928, its fascination with Mexican modernism was signaled as early as 1932 by the decision to take the first retrospective of Diego Rivera's work to tour the United States. Two energetic and visionary curators arrived at the Museum within the next decade: Henry Clifford in 1932 as first Assistant, then Associate, then full Curator of Paintings, and Carl Zigrosser in 1940 as Curator of Prints. Their passion for Mexican art would transform the collections of their respective departments during their tenures, both of which lasted until 1964.

It is thanks to Henry Clifford's energetic organization for Philadelphia of the ambitious exhibition *Mexican Art Today*, in 1943, that the Museum acquired many of its modern Mexican masterpieces as gifts from trustees and collectors. Clifford himself, together with his wife Esther, presented *The Dead Girl*, a celebrated early work by Juan Soriano, which has been in good part the inspiration for the present exhibition.

With masterworks by Diego Rivera, David Alfaro Siqueiros, and Rufino Tamayo, this Museum's rich collection of Mexican modernism comprises paintings, drawings, and a large and distinguished holding of prints, and encompasses important work by artists less well known in the United States but deserving of greater recognition. Prime among them is Juan Soriano, of whose early work the Museum owns four examples. Soriano's friendship over thirty years with Henry Clifford accounts in part for the archival resources of which guest curator and scholar Edward J. Sullivan of New York University has made such cogent use in his essay that follows. Professor Sullivan commands a remarkable breadth of knowledge in the field of Latin American Studies, and the Museum is grateful for his enthusiastic consent to undertake this project despite its compressed schedule. We also thank Carlos Fuentes and Marie José Paz, widow of Octavio Paz, for their kind permission to reprint two important texts on Soriano.

It is a delight to present Soriano's distinctive art to American museumgoers at a time that coincides with the Philadelphia presentation of the traveling retrospective of his friend Frida Kahlo, organized by the Walker Art Center and the San Francisco Museum of Modern Art in celebration of the artist's centennial. In Philadelphia, Michael R. Taylor, The Muriel and Philip Berman Curator of Modern Art, ably assisted by Emily Hage, have collaborated with Edward Sullivan on the presentation of the Soriano exhibition. We are grateful to Telcel, the Fundación José Cuervo, and a generous anonymous benefactor, who have made this Soriano project possible, and to the lenders in Mexico and the United States whose passion for Soriano's art has allowed this relatively small exhibition to have such a powerful impact. A special debt of gratitude is owed to Marek Keller, whose wholehearted enthusiasm for this project from its inception has enabled its realization.

ANNE D'HARNONCOURT
The George D. Widener Director and Chief Executive Officer

Author's Acknowledgments

My greatest debt of gratitude is to Marek Keller, director of the Fundación Juan Soriano y Marek Keller A.C., Mexico City, for his kindness and assistance with every phase of this project. At the Philadelphia Museum of Art, Director Anne d'Harnoncourt was gracious and encouraging from the beginning, as were Michael R. Taylor and Emily Hage of the Department of Modern and Contemporary Art, and Suzanne F. Wells and Zoe Kahr of the Department of Special Exhibitions. Archivist Susan K. Anderson, Curatorial Associate Ella B. Schaap, and Josephine Albarelli were generous with their invaluable information. In the Publishing Department, Sherry Babbitt edited the text with careful attention, Richard Bonk oversaw the production of images for the catalogue, and David Updike contributed valuable observations during the last stages of the manuscript's preparation. I also gratefully acknowledge the following individuals for their critically important contributions to my research and the success of this project: Andrés Blaisten, Renata Lia Blaisten González, James Oles, and Edith Fey of the Museo Andrés Blaisten, Mexico City; Alfonso Miranda Márquez, Héctor Palhares Mesa, and Pablo Berrocal of the Museo Soumaya, Mexico City; the administrative staff of the Gilcrease Museum, Tulsa, Oklahoma; Cathy Curry and Geaninne Guimarães of The Museum of Modern Art, New York; Taína Caragol of the University of Essex; Margarita Aguilar of Christie's, New York; Dr. Susan Aberth of Bard College, New York; Mariana Pérez Amor of the Galería de Arte Mexicano, Mexico City; Malú Block of the Galería Juan Martín, Mexico City; Roberto Márquez and Ana Saldamondo; Dr. Clara Bargellini of the Instituto de Investigaciones Estéticas, Universidad Autónoma de México, Mexico City; and Clayton C. Kirking of The New York Public Library.

Lenders to the Exhibition

Fundación Juan Soriano y Marek Keller A.C., Mexico City
Gilcrease Museum, Tulsa, Oklahoma
Museo Andrés Blaisten, Mexico City
Museo Soumaya, Mexico City
The Museum of Modern Art, New York

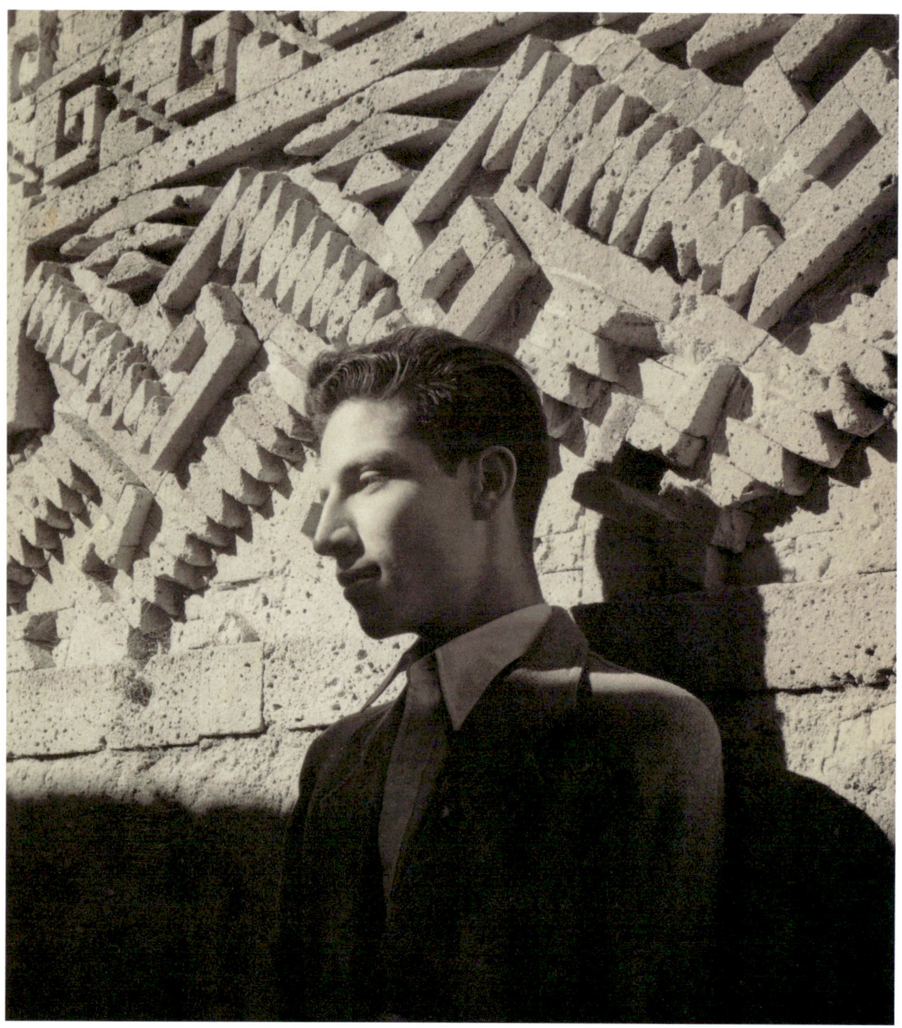

Lola Alvarez Bravo (Mexican, 1907–1993). *Portrait of Juan Soriano*, c. 1937–38. Photograph, 5⅛ x 4¾ inches (13 x 12.1 cm). Fundación Juan Soriano y Marek Keller A.C., Mexico City. Courtesy Center for Creative Photography, University of Arizona.

The Faces of Juan Soriano

Octavio Paz

Light body, made of bones as fragile as the skeletons in the toy shop, slightly bent over, who knows if by experience or forebodings; large and bony puppet hands, uneloquent; narrow shoulders that recall the stone wings of an angel or the membranes of a bat; thin fickle neck, guarded by a stiff starched collar; and the face: a bird, a lost orphan colt. Seeming older, a boy dressed like a man. Or a bird disguised as a human. Or a colt that was a bird and a boy and an old man, all at the same time. Or, in the end, simply an eternal child, ageless, bitter, cynical, naive, malicious, hardened, helpless.

Ancient boy, petrified, intelligent, passionate, fantastic, real. A boy conscious of his boyhood, repenting his boyhood, mercilessly attacking his boyhood, armed with all the weapons of the adults and none of their hypocrisy, virtue, childishness: he does not know the preservation instinct. (An instinct that is not born with a man: it is created by hopes, ambitions, fears, triumphs, age.)

With the cruelty and candor tossed off by boys and the wary experience of older men, he wounds his childhood. From that wound sprout mysterious beings: "monkeys" almost like children, on the verge of saying something; "girls from the slums," petrified or laboriously dancing in a solid air that suffocates them; paper flowers, fruits of stone, animals related by blood or marriage: flies, chameleons, small reptiles, birds, squirrels; wooden doors—what sad childhood, what tears or what loneliness lies behind them?—and balconies and hallways where solitary children run, always at the point of falling in the patio.

Between his work and those who contemplate it there is a contact, a shock, at times a repulsion, and always an answer. His drawing is sometimes harsh, anguished; his colors, sour. What is he looking for or trying to express? Is he seeking that boyhood he hates, like a lover knocking at the heart's door? He reveals a childhood, a paradise, flower and thorn, lost to emotions and intelligence, but one that eternally springs, not like the water from a fountain, but like the blood from a wound. He reveals to us, and reveals to himself, a part of our intimacy, of our being. The darkest, smallest, most hidden; perhaps the most powerful.

[Mexico City, August 1941]

Translated by Eliot Weinberger

The Eye of Dawn: Juan Soriano

Carlos Fuentes

In the 1960s I published a short story, "Doll Queen." As I wrote it, I thought I was remembering a disturbing scene that my friends and I saw on Lerma Street in Mexico City: a hall illuminated by candles surrounding a white coffin where a dead little girl slept. A porcelain doll suffocated by flowers and satin.

When morning came, it would all vanish. At night, it would reappear. I thought my story was a literary translation of that mysterious reality until one day my wife, Silvia, and I walked into a Gustave Courbet retrospective at the Petit Palais in Paris.

There we found a painting, *The Preparation of the Bride*: a young woman being prepared for her wedding, surrounded by diligent maids of honor. But that painting actually conceals another one, also by Courbet, called *The Dead Bride*. Here the maids of honor are dressing a bride, not for her wedding, but for her funeral.

Courbet's pentimento—the transferal of his moral will to daylight, bestowing his night on life—suddenly made me remember that before I wrote "Doll Queen," before I ever saw the porcelain girl night after night, I'd seen a painting—the first I'd ever seen by Juan Soriano. A disturbing painting, suspended on the edge of repentance, called *The Dead Girl*.

Now I'm writing a story derived from Courbet's pentimento, but this time I know that behind it, like a spectral drawing, is not another story, not an experience I had on Lerma Street, but another painting. Soriano precedes Courbet. Writing is dreaming—I always knew that—but so is painting. And originality is the art of returning to origins without revealing it.

I bring up these things to say that at the heart of Juan Soriano's art lies a mystery, one that all of us who enjoy his painting are responsible for sustaining. But neither Soriano nor his admirers could keep that mystery alive. It's the mystery of dawn: Soriano precedes Courbet because he reiterates the experience of another painter. But that reiteration establishes the community of art at its origin: Soriano leads to Courbet and to Courbet's origin, which is the origin of painting.

In a stunning essay on Soriano, the Spanish philosopher María Zambrano says that his painting wants "to be dawning itself." "Every true painting is in a cave, in solitude and silence." Through the mouth of the cave "our blind and hidden being" comes into the world and finally sees it. Every work of art, Zambrano says, reiterates its origin.

Because these stages of the origin—to be dawning, to leave the cave, to organize life, to fix ourselves in the orbit that "rescues and sustains" the most diverse creatures by unifying them—are an act of the origin. But it is also a repeated act of the present, and, foreseeably, an act that constitutes the future.

Octavio Barreda, who met Soriano when he was a very young boy just arrived in Mexico City from Guadalajara, saw him as a demonic child who brought El Greco's colors to Mexican painting only because he'd never seen them: He'd dreamed them. Soriano dreams El Greco's colors before seeing them. That's why he precedes Courbet; that's why he heralds Bonnard. The dilemma of any artistic intelligence is how to be faithful to its origin (tradition, birthright, filiation, and foundation; painting being painting in order to be everything else, but never the other way around) without betraying its own flight, its desire, its hunger for a future. The dilemma is always resolved in the present, which is the time of the picture itself: Only in that place is the origin remembered and destiny desired.

Soriano, like all great painters, is present in this present that doesn't sacrifice its past or its future. But the peculiar magic—the mystery—of his art is that in it Soriano makes us feel it is present, that it evokes its origin and projects its future. Soriano in himself is a dawning: a beginning charged with past, a daybreak that does not deceive us with the promise of an innocent future.

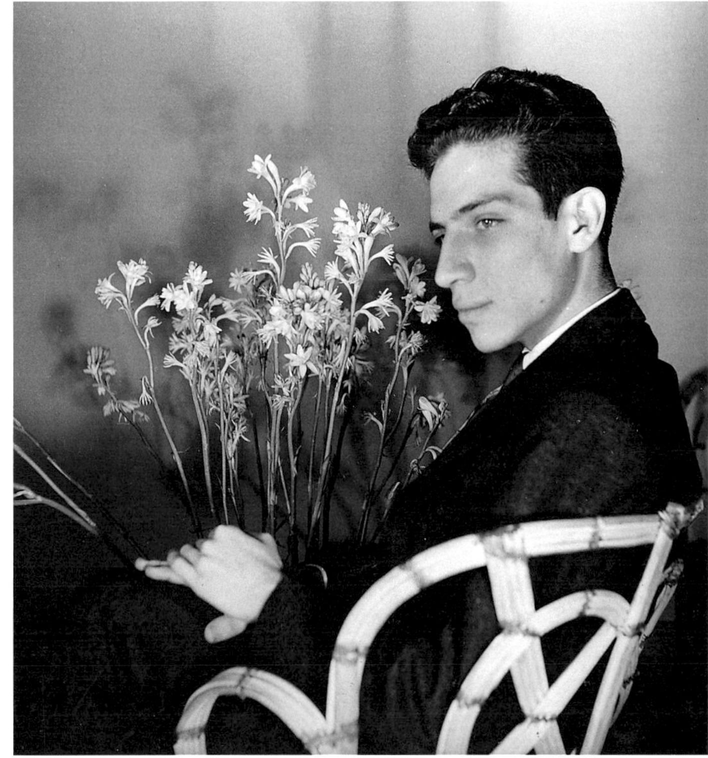

Lola Alvarez Bravo. *Juan Soriano with Flowers*, c. 1937–38. Photograph, 5 x 4⅞ inches (12.7 x 12.4 cm). Fundación Juan Soriano y Marek Keller A.C., Mexico City. Courtesy Center for Creative Photography, University of Arizona. © 1995 The University of Arizona Foundation

Juan Soriano's painting is a wound in the cavern. Before many, sometimes alone among many, he ran the risk of reinventing the figures of painting by giving the impression of a rift, of a restarting, of vacillations, of radical change. All that was respectable, even daring and most certainly historical: Picasso. Was he only eclectic? Was Soriano only giving us a brilliant outpouring of jewels without a crown in which to set them? What was the mystery of this work, sometimes so exciting, other times so tight, so fluid, adventurous, ambulating, and sometimes mercurial?

How many times did Soriano reach his peak? How many times did he abandon his safe mountaintop and throw himself, a hero of gravity, into an abyss from which he emerged neither suffering nor joyful but different, covered with different skin, crowned with thorns and roses, aerial like his baroque angels, but sometimes obscure, like an animal singed by the immediacy of a Nahuatl hell painted with the green mud of subtropical canyons, tinted at times with the pure light of a romantic lightning flash against the backdrop of a classical theater? But, and this always: an art of sexual pleasure, fornicart, art of incitements, incitart, art of sumptuous fugues, fugart.

Today, no one can deny that Juan Soriano is a painter of elements and figures: elemental and figurative. And it is here in elements and figures where we find the crown for those jewels. Here is the synthesis of his diversity.

Benedetto Croce talks about a "pure intuition" in art, which would be elemental because it is authorial, an original budding or unfolding always alien to an abstraction that pure intuition knows nothing of but which already includes a totality of destinies, hopes, pains, delights, miseries, and human servitude—"the entire drama of reality perpetually evolving and growing out of its own self with suffering and joy."

Soriano's "pure intuition" has led him to repeat the origin without forgetting (and this is his irony) that it has its own history. Croce's hatred of artistic gratuitousness, which he attributes to Schiller, acquires in Soriano a permanent gravity. This painter, so varied, so "eclectic," so reinitiating, is always gravely, obstinately attached to the rite of the elements: Air and fire,

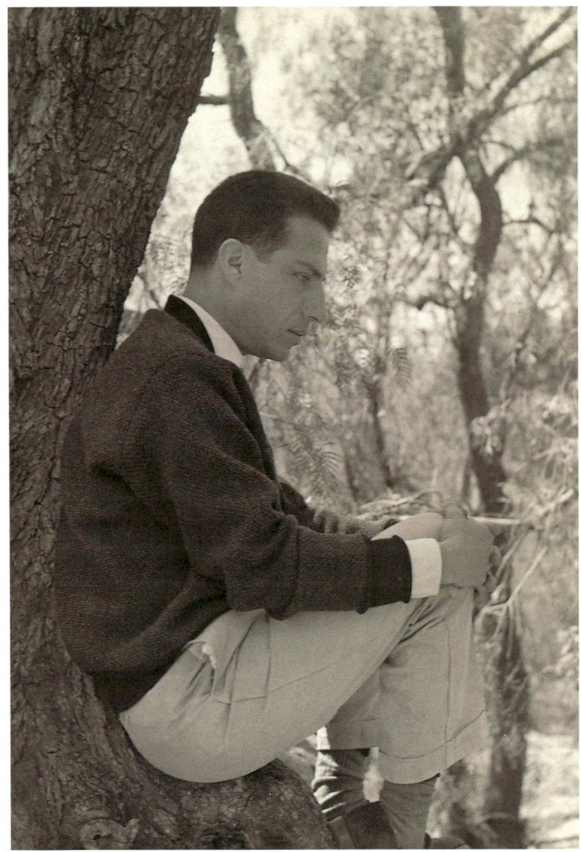

Lola Alvarez Bravo. *Portrait of Juan Soriano in Chapultepec Park, Mexico City,* 1947. Photograph, 7 x 5 inches (17.8 x 12.7 cm). Fundación Juan Soriano y Marek Keller A.C., Mexico City. Courtesy Center for Creative Photography, University of Arizona. © 1995 The University of Arizona Foundation

airart and fireart, water and earth, waterart and earthart are the fathers and mothers of Soriano's painting, and everything else descends from the elements, very rich, varied, but strung on the necklace of air and fire, water and earth. Angels and serpents, gods and bicyclists, lovers and toads, bulls and female friends of the painter, vases and coffins, lions and skulls, fish and saints. We never stop seeing them through, in, with, from his elements. The great portrait of Sofía and Ignacio Bernal [see fig. 2] is also a portrait of air and light. Apollo and the muses is also a painting of fire. The portrait of Lupe Marín is just as much a portrait of the earth she's planted on. And the recent *Crocodile* is also a profile of water.

Soriano illustrates Croce's maxim: Artistic expression includes the totality and reflects the cosmos through a wholly individual form.

Annunciation, dawn: Soriano reclaims for art/allart/hisart/hisartistry the privileges of knowledge. Art is not a form of knowledge or an auxiliary of logic: Art is knowledge. This identity is indispensable if "elemental" art is ever to become truly figurative art: not the representation or the reproduction of something, but the constitution of something.

Ultimately a friendly or contiguous spirit (familiar, sorcerer's apprentice; sorcererart), Soriano quickly understood in painting, just as the Argentine writer Julio Cortázar understood in literature, that the challenge is the figure, because there is nothing more forsaken, nothing blurrier, less identifiable, less propped up by reason or feeling than that nascent figure (serpent, dead girl, muse, bicyclist) that we yet don't know how to name, or even discern, and which, nevertheless, reading with Novalis and Henry James the invisible plot of the loom, we know to be essential: Identical to our own being, which is no longer that of the consecrated archetype or the psychological "round" character (demanded by E. M. Forster, who couldn't imagine a forgotten K., or a Beckettian being with no more dimension than the trash can he inhabits). The demand of the figure has become in our times a demand that puts us on the border between life and death. A being decides between life and death, claiming our imagination, our name, and our memory: It's the figure we catch by surprise in a painting by Soriano or a story by Cortázar, in all the nakedness of its constitutive abandonment: dawnlike, elemental.

We can no longer paint, love, or live any longer except with what appears, "dawning" its way through the cave and leaving its first track on the illuminated mud. Diego de Mesa tells of how when Soriano was a boy without an audience he would look into a mirror and put on shows for himself. It's the devil making faces in the image and likeness of . . . .

I think the rebel demon is waiting for the only reliable proof of the goodness of God: the forgiving of Lucifer, the end of hell.

And until such time as that happens, Soriano will continue to be a devil in the modest paradise of Mexico. I personally identify Soriano with moments of my life and moments of Mexican history, especially when his deepest friendships were formed. Diego de Mesa, María Zambrano, between the "subverted Eden," the

Mexico of López Velarde, and the "pilgrim Spain," fatigued and recognized, that took place in Mexico more than half a century ago.

In that unification of our "modest homeland" with the fugitive homeland of Spain, we recognized the coming together of New World renovations and European continuities. In that dawnlike instant when Mexico finally recognized an intelligent Spain and stopped being the bastard of conquering Spain, both—Europeans and New World citizens—took on a collective obligation: Neither side would any longer be owners—we would stop owning our utopian identity, and Europeans would stop owning their civilizing identity. Like Quevedo, "I cast my eyes on the walls of my country." We were no longer, or, we still were not owners of a language, a profile, a tradition. We were making all of those things. We were dawning, Spaniards and Mexicans together, obliged to recover by inventing: to win ourselves by imagining ourselves.

This time, artists decided that we would win identity, history, and language, with equal freedom for the giver and the receiver. Perhaps this is the question posed by Juan Soriano, the eminent and inventive actor in that unification which took place in 1939: Are we capable of achieving the synthesis of those elements he has placed before our dazzled eyes, without waiting for the painter to do it for us, without confusing his respect for us with a weakness in the artist? Instead, it is his true strength: his ability to share the elements, help the figures, and deserve the annunciation.

This invitation remains Soriano's mystery: elemental figuration of the dawn; element; figure; waking. Wakeart.

Translated by Alfred Mac Adam

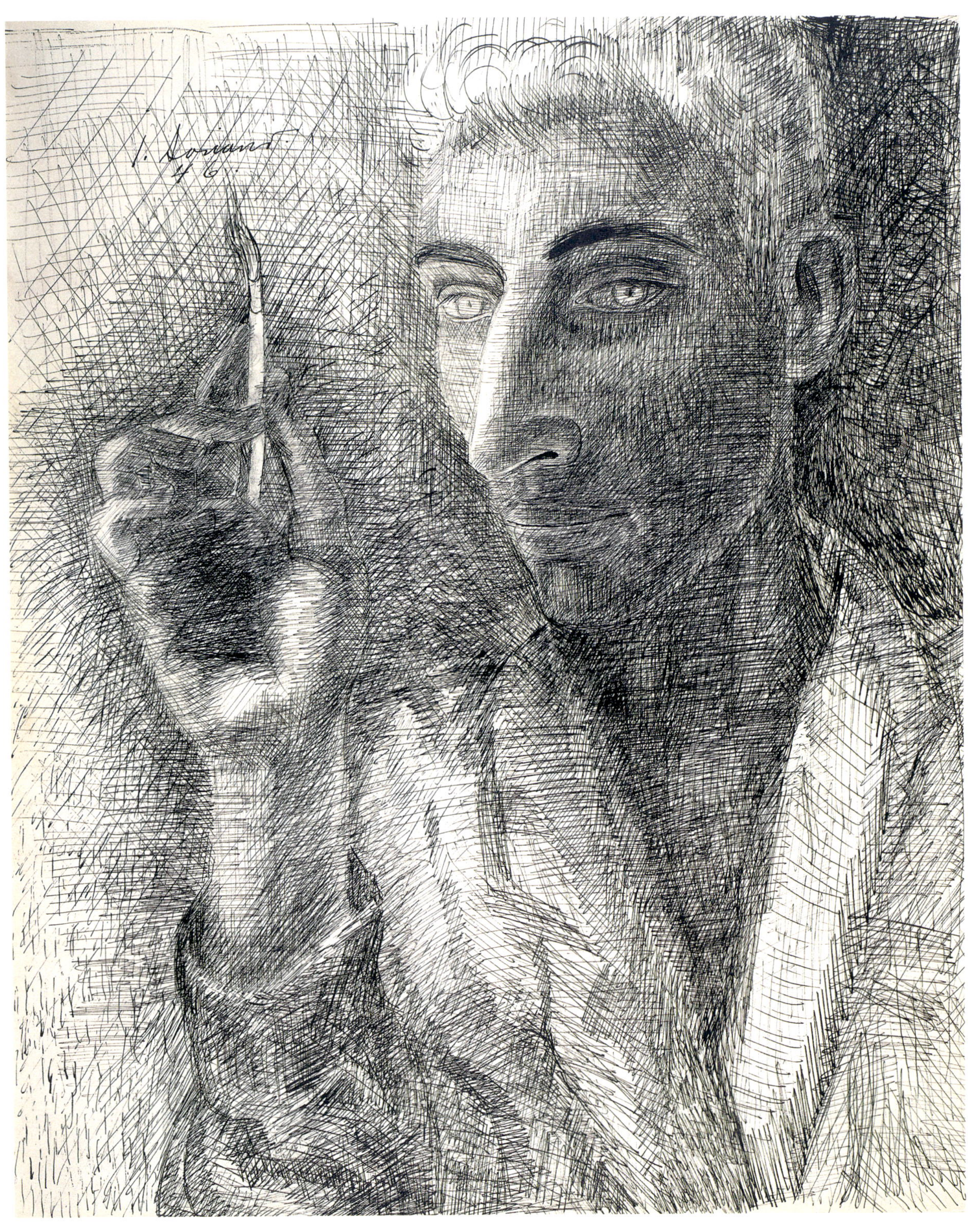

*FIG. 1. *Self-Portrait*, 1946. Ink on paper, 15 3/16 x 12 3/4 inches (38.6 x 32.4 cm). Museo Soumaya, Mexico City

Fragile Demon: Juan Soriano in Mexico, 1935 to 1950

Edward J. Sullivan

Introduction

Juan Soriano (1920–2006) had a distinguished career as a painter, printmaker, and sculptor that lasted from 1934 until virtually the time of his death. A younger contemporary of such famous Mexican artists as Diego Rivera, Frida Kahlo, and José Clemente Orozco, Soriano, seen here in a dreamily evocative self-portrait drawing from 1946 (fig. 1),[1] is celebrated at home but is much less well known abroad. There has not been, until now, a show dedicated to his early years in his native Guadalajara and Mexico City, where he lived from 1935 to 1951 before departing for an extended period in Europe. This volume is published on the occasion of the first monographic exhibition of Soriano's work in a major U.S. institution, and the Philadelphia Museum of Art is an appropriate organizer of such an effort for several reasons. In the 1940s, the Museum's Curator of Paintings Henry Clifford was actively involved in collecting modern Mexican painting, and he was instrumental in acquiring Philadelphia's four Sorianos from this period, the largest number in any U.S. institution. One of these, the compellingly mysterious *Dead Girl* of 1938 (see fig. 36), has become a virtually iconic image, appearing in books and exhibitions as the quintessential example of its genre. The Museum's other works by Soriano—*Still Life* of 1942 (see fig. 12), *Girl with a Mask* of 1945 (see fig. 35), and *Girl with Bouquet* of 1946 (see fig. 13)—are representative of the principal themes of his art during these years. The Museum's strong collection of colonial and twentieth-century Mexican painting, long-standing commitment to exhibiting Latin American art,[2] and distinguished holdings of international modern art similarly make it an especially fitting venue for the project.

Why is Juan Soriano not better known outside Mexico? One reason may be that he did not have consistent gallery representation as an emerging artist. Although he was on cordial terms with the renowned art dealer Inés Amor of the Galería de Arte Mexicano in Mexico City, he had only two solo shows there in the 1940s, and he never had a formal contract with the gallery. In contrast to many of his contemporaries, who engaged in aggressive marketing, Soriano was not a self-promoter. Also unlike many of the most successful Mexican painters of the years before and immediately after World War II, his politics were not leftist, and thus he did not receive (nor did he seek) official, public commissions that were so often given to others on the basis of political affiliation.

During the 1930s and 1940s, the years to which Philadelphia's works date, Soriano developed a realistic mode of expression in his paintings of children, still lifes, portraits, and allegories. This vision was tinged with what some critics have labeled romanticism, and others have dubbed "Surrealist tendencies." While there are a number of monographs and specialized studies of his work, Soriano has yet to be the subject of the type of revisionist appraisal that a younger generation of Mexican and non-Mexican scholars has focused on many other key figures of this period.[3] Looking anew at this important modern master with a view toward situating him more securely within the larger panorama of his time, both within Mexico and abroad, will serve to unveil new, long-needed critical perspectives on his work.

Soriano in Guadalajara

Reminiscing about his early years Soriano stated:

> Nothing affected my life more than those first fifteen years in Guadalajara. Nothing that has happened to me since has been more important than [the state of] Jalisco. I learned all the oral traditions. My father and mother wanted to make me into a son of the Revolution. They smothered me with their memories of battles, . . . cries of the clarinet, [military] camps, cheers for the Revolution, locomotives, and attempted assassinations.[4]

Although he rarely spent time in Guadalajara after leaving for Mexico City in 1935, the culture of this conservative city served as the basis for many of the themes and details of his work during the period under consideration here. Soriano was born on August 18, 1920 (the year that marked the end of the Mexican Revolution), into a family of thirteen aunts and four sisters. He was the youngest child and the only male sibling. His father, Rafael Rodríguez Soriano, was a minor politician who had fought in the Revolution and whose wife, Amalia Montoya, had followed him into battle.

Soriano was a solitary child who spent long periods in convalescence from his many illnesses. His sisters, especially Rosa and Martha, were instrumental in encouraging him to express his fantasies in drawing and painting. Martha, ten years older than Juan, played a vital role in his life for many years, serving as muse and facilitator of her brother's earliest connections with local artists, most importantly Jesús Reyes Ferreira (known as Chucho Reyes). Reyes was a multifaceted personality who collected antiques, sold nineteenth-century Mexican paintings (including some fakes manufactured by the students of his informal classes, among them Soriano[5]), and ultimately established a distinguished career as an artist, usually of small, rapidly painted images of animals, skeletons, or fantastic creatures in ink or watercolor on rice paper. Chucho Reyes fostered the young painter's interest in Mexican folk art as well as the popular traditions of nineteenth-century portraiture.

It was Reyes who introduced Soriano to the world of art beyond the confines of the city and country. His substantial library contained many books on the masters of the Italian and Northern Renaissance. He subscribed to newspapers and magazines from abroad that carried images of the latest trends in art, all of which proved to be revelatory for the precocious child. Reyes also purchased some of Soriano's first paintings and drawings in order to resell them.[6] The theme of at least one of these paintings, a dead child, became a subject later repeated by Soriano in a number of his works (see figs. 36, 38, 42).[7]

Reyes was not the only person with whom the young Soriano studied in Guadalajara. His sister Martha enrolled him in the drawing classes of the local painter Francisco Rodríguez, whose studio, known as Evolución, was frequented by Agustín Lazo, Jesús Guerrero Galván, and others. After Soriano's move to Mexico City he kept up his contact with these and other artists from Jalisco and especially with the Guadalajara contingent, who in the 1940s formed a group with a particular visual ethos that the art historian Olivier Debroise has described as "a lyrical vein, a poetic inspiration which is a bit old-fashioned (provincial . . . if we take away its negative connotations), which some will soon misinterpret as Surrealism."[8] Inés Amor later supported many of these artists and made her Galería de Arte Mexicano a focal point for their artistic production.[9]

The cultural critic Carlos Monsiváis lyrically evoked the artistic atmosphere of Guadalajara in the earlier twentieth century, which continued to nourish the Jalisco group even after their move away from the city. Writing specifically of Soriano, he stated:

> Guadalajara was the center for the preservation of an aesthetic (called by [the poet Ramón] López Velarde), *la patria íntima*, which rejected the innovations of the capital of the Republic, judging them to be heretical, reverting [instead] to a past of colors, melodies, architectonic forms, oral culture, refrains, events, objects. Soriano attributes his creative predisposition and his scheme of values to the city of his birth.[10]

The reverberating influences of Soriano's native city included the religious processions that marked the ecclesiastical calendar, the home altars that were inevitable features of virtually every domestic setting, and especially the colonial architecture that still abounded in his youth. The artist recalled his attraction to these buildings—including churches, convents, and baronial residences—and their interiors: "I used to love to go into those colonial buildings, especially the churches. I would often wait until most of the people were leaving and then spend as long as possible looking at the altarpieces and the sculptures when the daylight was gradually disappearing."[11] This interest in seventeenth- and eighteenth-century art became more pronounced when the artist moved to Mexico City. His compositions of the 1940s often include figures of angels, both lifelike and sculptural, which even find their way into some of Soriano's formal portraits, such as the 1948

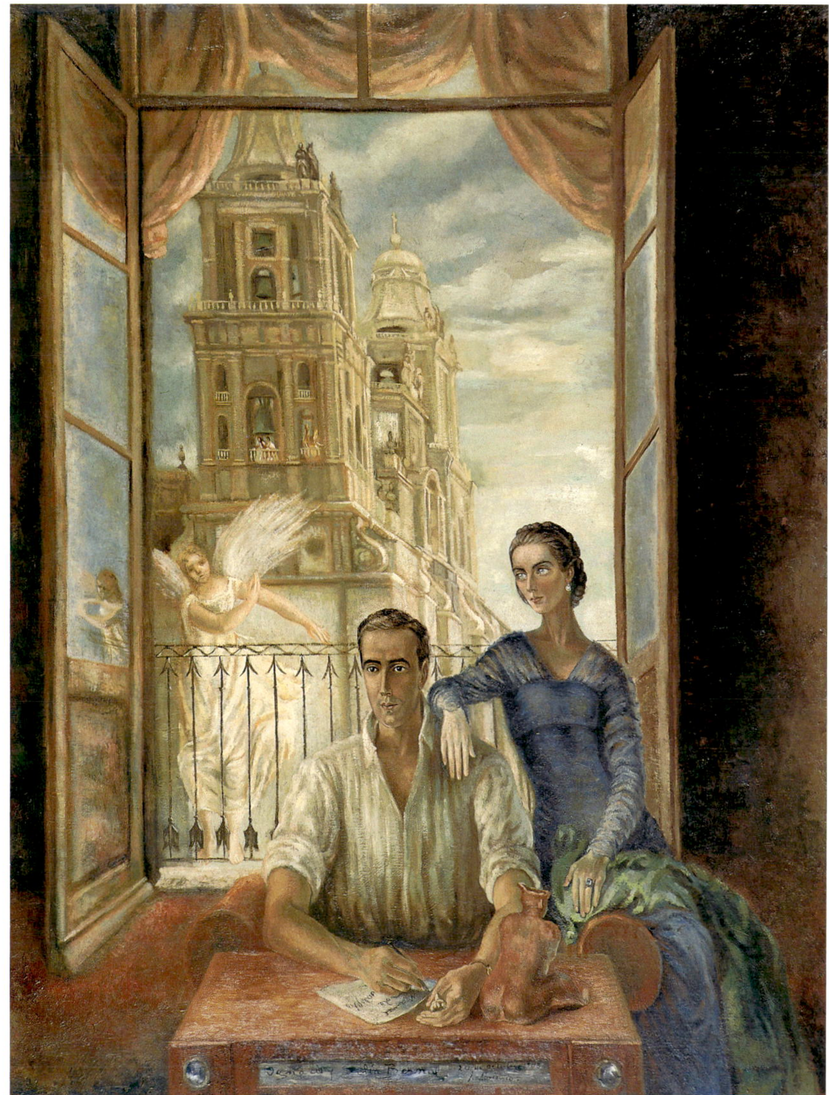

FIG. 2. *Portrait of Ignacio and Sofía Bernal*, 1948. Oil on canvas, 38³⁄₁₆ x 29⅞ inches (97 x 76 cm). Private collection. Courtesy of the Fundación Juan Soriano y Marek Keller A.C., Mexico City

Portrait of Ignacio and Sofía Bernal (fig. 2), in which the archaeologist of Monte Alban, Oaxaca, is seen with his wife against an open window with the bell towers of the Mexico City cathedral clearly visible and a large angel standing on the window ledge.

The Guadalajara painter Alfonso Michel was the first established artist to appreciate Soriano's watercolors when they were brought to his attention by his sister Martha.[12] There are several surviving portraits of the many that Soriano did of his sisters and their Guadalajara friends. The 1934 *Portrait of Martha* (fig. 3), which was painted in Rodríguez's studio, is a curious depiction (not unlike the Hollywood publicity shots of starlets of the time) of the upper portion of the sitter's body against a muddy yellow background. Her head is at the right, and at the left is a wedge of the blue table on which there are several books, one with the partially concealed title *La Farsa*. There is also a bottle of tequila because, as Soriano said, "Martha, like everyone else, drank a lot."[13] The artist explained that in this work "I sought . . . to produce a very strict composition. I liked to practice . . . dividing the space geometrically. . . . I had never thought that Cubism was of interest to me; I didn't like its bottles and

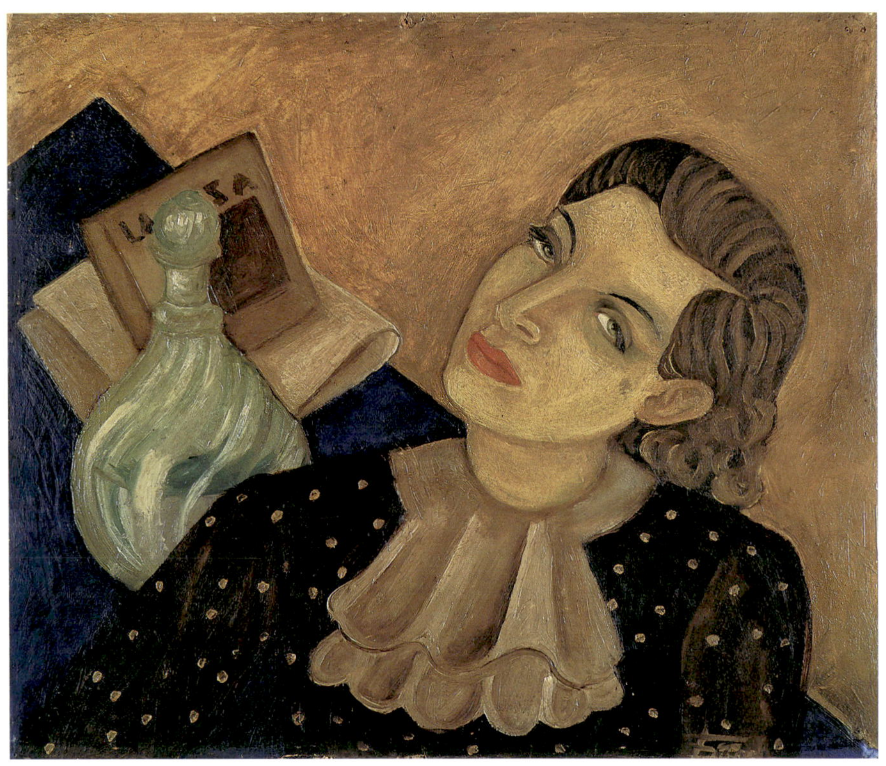

FIG. 3. *Portrait of Martha*, 1934. Oil on cardboard, 18½ x 22⁷⁄₁₆ inches (47 x 57 cm). Private collection. Courtesy of the Fundación Juan Soriano y Marek Keller A.C., Mexico City

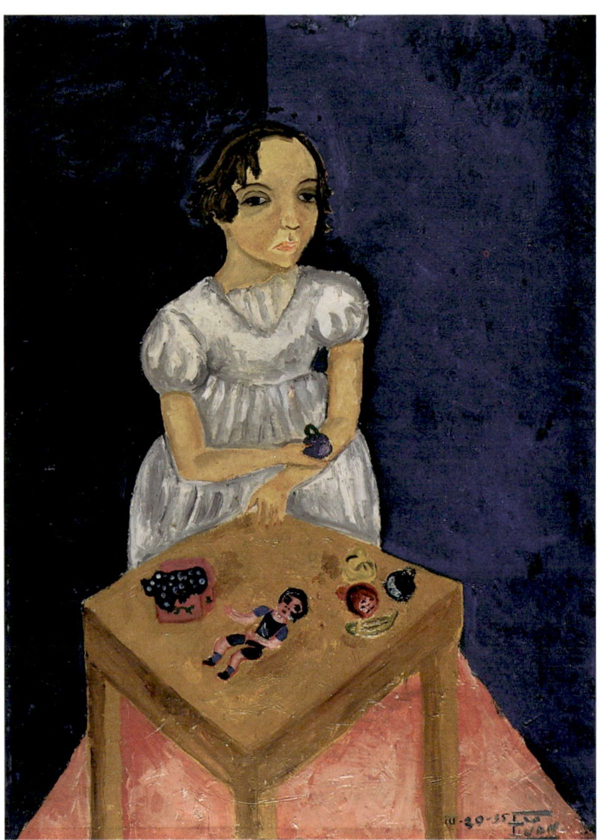

FIG. 4. *Portrait of a Girl*, 1935. Oil on cardboard, 18⅝ x 13¾ inches (47.3 x 35 cm). Fundación Juan Soriano y Marek Keller A.C., Mexico City

Cubist guitars, but when I go back and look at these first portraits I see that even though I wasn't conscious of it, there is a Cubist influence."[14] Painted in March 1935, the *Portrait of a Girl* (fig. 4) is a similar but somewhat more complex study of spatial division, with its background separated into two distinct, almost equal zones, both dark blue. The floor is a triangular shape of pink and the table a yellow rectangle. The girl herself is formed by interlocking, tubular shapes. On the table there are fruits, a flower, a bunch of grapes, a box, and a small papier-mâché doll, all resting somewhat uneasily on the surface.

While it would be fair to call these early pictures examples of juvenilia, they are significant indicators of the styles and techniques that Soriano was developing while still in Guadalajara and that continued to be useful to him later. His interest in the popular or folk forms to which he had been introduced by Chucho Reyes is evidenced in the 1935 portrait by the flat colors and elemental shapes of the objects on the table. We are equally reminded of the drawing method based on popular forms derived by the painter Adolfo Best Maugard and disseminated throughout Mexico (and abroad) through a state-published manual known to most children and art students in this period.[15] Yet Soriano ultimately digested and transformed these (perhaps even unconscious) sources to produce an art in the later 1930s and throughout the 1940s that, while making reference to certain visual foundations, radiated a high degree of sophistication and originality.

The youthful painter's "big break" came in 1934, when Soriano was brought to the attention of a group of well-established artists by Francisco Rodríguez's exhibition of his students' work at the Museo Regional de Guadalajara. During a visit to the show the photographer Lola Alvarez Bravo and the painters María Izquierdo and José Chávez Morado were struck by Soriano's paintings (many of which were on modest-size pieces of cardboard that a tailor uncle had given him) and urged the boy to broaden his horizons by moving to Mexico City. When in the capital, Soriano remained close to both Alvarez Bravo and Izquierdo.

Lola Alvarez Bravo became the artist's muse and model for a number of key works of the late 1930s and 1940s (a role that Guadalupe Marín, former wife of Diego Rivera, would play in the 1960s). Among these is the evocative 1944 double portrait of *Lola Alvarez Bravo with Juan Soriano as a Child* (fig. 5). Alvarez Bravo took many of the most significant photographic portraits of the artist, while also employing his image in some experimental pieces, such as her photomontages of the 1940s.[16] Izquierdo, whose work of the 1930s bears a marked similarity in subject and style to that of Soriano, also continued to play a pivotal role in his life. She painted one of the best known and most beautiful portraits of the young artist in 1939 (now in the Museo Andrés Blaisten, Mexico City), which was included (along with other likenesses of the painter's literary and artistic friends) in her solo show organized the same year at the Galería de Arte Mexicano.[17] Soriano said to the writer Elena Poniatowska that "María Izquierdo was fundamental [to me. She was] bewitching and had a very particular sense of humor. What a fabulous face of an antique sculpture!"[18]

Soriano in Mexico City

Soriano and the Literary Vanguard

On August 15, 1945, three days before Juan Soriano's twenty-fifth birthday, the Mexican poet, essayist, critic, and editor Octavio G. Barreda published a profile of the artist in his literary journal *El hijo pródigo*. Simply entitled "Juan Soriano," it offered a sketch of what the writer considered the artist's main physical and artistic traits. It begins by stating: "In 1920 was born this fragile, sickly demon." It then continues to evoke the times and artistic temperament of Mexico at the outset of the third decade of the century through an ironic allusion to the principal players in the country's postrevolutionary artistic scene, including the so-called Tres Grandes: Diego Rivera, José Clemente Orozco, and David Alfaro Siqueiros. "Soriano was born," Barreda wrote, "precisely at the moment when the grave and corpulent angels and archangels installed and opened to the public the dramatic panorama of our revolutionary renaissance. There, amidst that cardboard world, that [world of] stage scenery, of great barbarous curtains, of gigantic Wagnerian backdrops, this thin devil, this strange impertinent creature first saw the light of day."[19]

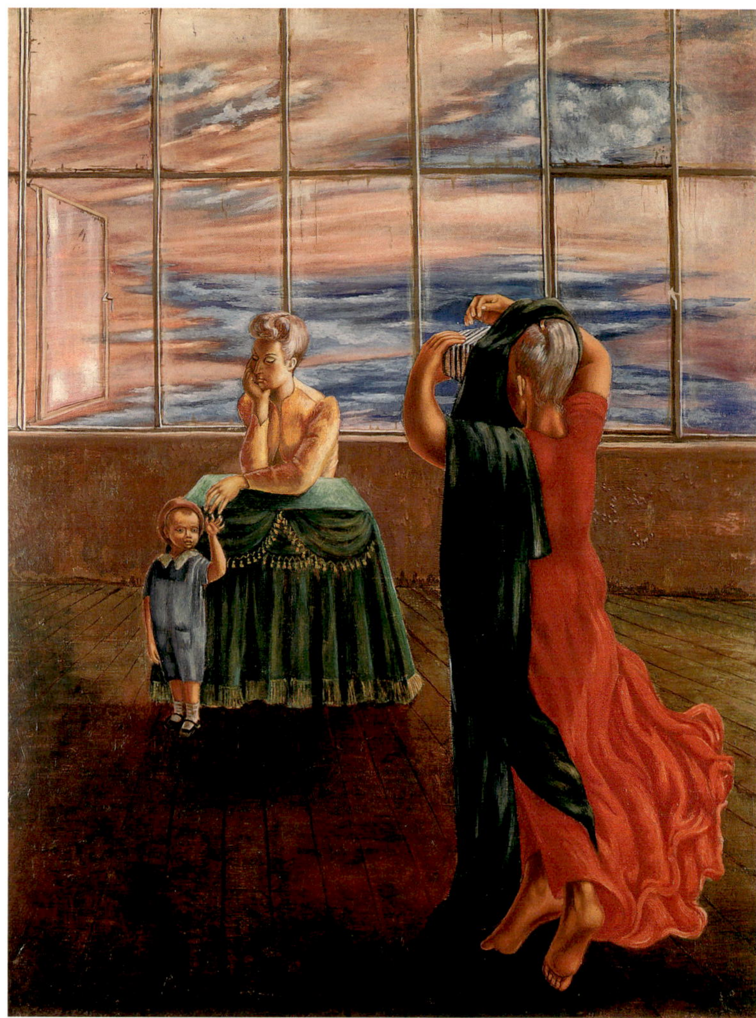

FIG. 5. *Portrait of Lola Alvarez Bravo with Juan Soriano as a Child*, 1944. Oil on canvas, 41⁵⁄₁₆ x 32⅝ inches (105 x 83 cm). Private collection. Courtesy of the Fundación Juan Soriano y Marek Keller A.C., Mexico City

After hinting at the growing conflicts within the Mexican art world, Barreda places Soriano within a context of his fellow artists:

> In fact, this diminutive devil is a friend and contemporary of [Ricardo] Martínez, a kindred spirit of Frida Kahlo, [Agustín] Lazo, [Rufino] Tamayo, [Carlos] Mérida and other principal inhabitants of the subterranean worlds. [He is] of frail stature, somewhat short and thin, with a long nose; with skin and hair dyed to an almost-imperceptible old gold, skittish in the manner of a strange bird, perhaps, one of Disney's woodpeckers.[20]

The introductory paragraphs of this biographical sketch, while seemingly jocular, actually reveal several significant points about the artist. The first is, of course, the impression of his physical state ("diminutive," "frail"), with the addition of his mischievous (or even devilish) qualities. Many essays on the personality and art of Soriano written between the late 1930s and the mid-1940s emphasize his youth, and he is often referred to as a "child." This is not surprising, as he began to exhibit at age fourteen. More importantly, though, Barreda gingerly inserts Soriano within the artistic camp opposed to the politically and socially engaged art that characterized Mexican muralism and its principal proponents, and links him instead to some of the main protagonists of the various countermovements that had begun to assert themselves in the later 1930s and 1940s. Artists such as Tamayo and Martínez practiced a type of figuration mostly devoid of the facile trappings of *mexicanidad* ("Mexican-ness") that characterized much of the visual production of the so-called Mexican School.[21]

By associating the names of Kahlo, Lazo, and Mérida with Soriano, Barreda connects all of them to a particular type of painting in Mexico in the first half of the 1940s, which is often related to Surrealism.

Four years before Barreda wrote his description of Soriano, the Mexican poet and essayist Octavio Paz published his own evocation of the young man (see page 9). Paz's essay, one of many he would write about Soriano, was certainly not the first to concentrate on the accomplishments of the youthful artist, but in his text he employed the most lyrical language used to date to describe his achievements as well as his physical persona: "Light body, made of bones as fragile as the skeletons in the toy shop. . . . Ancient boy, petrified, intelligent, passionate, fantastic, real."[22] Paz was twenty-seven years old when he wrote these lines about his friend, who was then only twenty-one. The two met when Paz returned from Spain in 1938, after working for a year for the Republican government as a propagandist during the Spanish Civil War. They remained lifelong friends despite long separations while Paz took on various postings to Mexican embassies abroad.[23]

It was virtually predestined that some of the strongest relationships Soriano formed in his early years would be with poets, novelists, and playwrights. He has stated that reading novels and attending theatrical performances were among his first passions as a child.[24] After Soriano's move to Mexico City in 1935, both literature and his friendships with the members of the group of vanguard poets and essayists known as the Contemporáneos became an integral part of his social and artistic life. Soriano told Elena Poniatowska that

> Octavio Barreda (for whom I made a few drawings for *El hijo pródigo*, which he edited) and [the poet] Xavier Villaurrutia gave me access to their library, and the books taught me new ways of seeing the world. Octavio Barreda explained to me what I didn't know. Poetry took on an immense role in my life, and it has become enormous with time. In the 1930s, I suddenly found in a poem by Villaurrutia or Paz the answer to things in life I didn't understand.[25]

The route of inspiration ran equally in the opposite direction; Paz later remarked that "the influence of Soriano has been decisive not only among painters and sculptors, but also on theater and poetry."[26]

Theater was of exceptional importance for Soriano, and he did some of his most important ephemeral work for various theatrical companies in Mexico City from the late 1930s until well into the 1950s. Indeed, many of his paintings from the years considered here reflect his engagement with the stage (see figs. 26, 29, 41). His interest in designing sets and costumes for productions of contemporary as well as classical dramas had its origins in his childhood fascination with the theater in his native Guadalajara. As a boy Soriano had been fascinated by puppets and often created his own tiny stages from boxes and cartons. He began to make figures from wax and clay, and, later, as a young man in Mexico City, he continued to foster this element of his creativity. In Guadalajara, the Soriano family lived near the Teatro Principal, which the young boy would often visit to meet the actors and, ultimately, help the stagehands paint flats in exchange for free admission to performances.[27]

Beginning in 1938 Soriano worked for several theater companies in the capital. In that year he created his first sets, for a production of the classic drama *El tejedor de Segovia* (The Weaver of Segovia) by the late-sixteenth–early-seventeenth-century Mexican playwright Juan Ruiz de Alarcón at the Teatro del Sindicato de Electrisistas. The following year he began working on scenery and costumes for a variety of (mostly classical) plays at the Teatro Orientación. Among his somewhat older fellow artists (many of whom were associated with the Contemporáneos) who had also worked at this theater earlier in the 1930s were Tamayo, Julio Castellanos, Lazo, and Antonio Ruiz. While working at the Teatro Orientación, Soriano taught life drawing at the Escuela de Pintura y Escultura (called La Esmeralda), whose director was his friend Ruiz.[28]At the same time he frequented the ceramics workshop of the Costa Rican–born artist Francisco Zúñiga. The mythological subjects of these early (lost) works echoed his later interest in classical themes that by the 1950s became pervasive in his sculpture (in clay and ultimately bronze) and that continued to be of great importance to Soriano even into old age.

Soriano was likewise attracted to the ballet and

modern dance that had been flourishing in Mexico since the painter Adolfo Best Maugard designed sets for a folk ballet performed by Ana Pavlova in a Mexico City bullring in 1919.[29] By the 1930s there were a number of distinguished Mexican-born choreographers, some of whom became Soriano's friends and subjects of his many portraits done in the late 1930s and throughout the 1940s. Dancers such as Amalia Hernández (founder of the Ballet Folklórico de México) and Ana Mérida also commissioned Soriano to design costumes and sets for their performances. He was equally attracted by the most famous Mexican film stars of the 1940s, becoming particularly friendly with Dolores del Río and María Félix, whose portrait he drew in 1959.[30]

In the late 1930s and into the 1940s Soriano participated in the meetings of various theatrical, literary, and artistic groups who gathered to discuss their work as well as to drink and gossip at the Café de París on the calle Cinco de Mayo in downtown Mexico City. They would also frequent more low-life bars such as El Tenampa on the calle Obregón, where Henri Cartier-Bresson had photographed his famous series of prostitutes. Most of the participants in these gatherings had been connected in one way or another with the Contemporáneos, including Villaurrutia, Barreda, Salvador Novo, Lazo, Carlos Pellicer, Gilberto Owen, and Rafael Solana.

By the time Soriano became identified with the Contemporáneos, the group (which was by no means a cohesive organization) had experienced a number of reconfigurations since its most active phase in the late 1920s. The philosophy of its liberal-minded adherents[31] was almost diametrically opposed to that of literary/artistic associations that flourished in the 1920s such as the Estridentistas and ¡30-30!, whose members exalted contemporaneity in their literary and visual images of aggressively "modern" factories, automobiles, and machines, as well as the muralists, centered around the Tres Grandes, who relied on socially charged iconography.[32] The Contemporáneos, by contrast, were committed to an experimental, non-nationalistic expression in their works. Some (although by no means all) of the members of the Contemporáneos were gay, and a homoerotic ethos permeated certain examples of their literary and visual production, including that by Soriano. This was an element to which many of their generation took exception, and it represented a point of challenge between the Contemporáneos and other Mexican artists and writers who acclaimed direct or implied representations of heterosexuality as the *sine qua non* of visual or literary expression.[33] Soriano's frank affirmation of his sexuality in his paintings, drawings, writings, and interviews would remain a hallmark of his personality throughout his life.[34]

While Soriano was candid about sexual matters, he was not necessarily liberal when it came to politics. In 1941 the Institute of Modern Art in Boston organized a traveling exhibition entitled *Modern Mexican Painters*.[35] Among the twenty-three artists included, Soriano was represented by a self-portrait done that same year. In the caption to the illustration in the catalogue, the U.S. art collector and writer MacKinley Helm stated that Soriano is "the favorite new painter of the conservative wing in Mexico,"[36] thus contrasting him to the social activists among the muralists and their cohort. Yet Soriano was not alone among his Mexican contemporaries in his aversion to overt political imagery and statements. His growing engagement with "universalist" themes, especially after his move to Rome in 1951, and his cultivation of classically oriented subject matter in his painting and sculpture were analogous to the sensibility of Paz and Tamayo, two men he much admired. Soriano was sympathetic to their conservative stance, which became more marked in all three of them in later decades.

Soriano and His Artistic Circle

Two of the many photographs of Juan Soriano taken by Alvarez Bravo throughout the late 1930s and 1940s are particularly strong indicators of the artist's friendships and activities after he moved to Mexico City in 1935. One of them (fig. 6) shows him in a suit, standing against a wall contemplating one of two conch shells hanging by wires. Conch shells figure prominently in some of Soriano's still lifes, as they did in those of such Mexican colleagues as Izquierdo, Tamayo, Siqueiros, and Manuel González Serrano. Their sensuous curves evoke not only the mysteries of the sea but female sexuality. Although the tone of this photo is serious

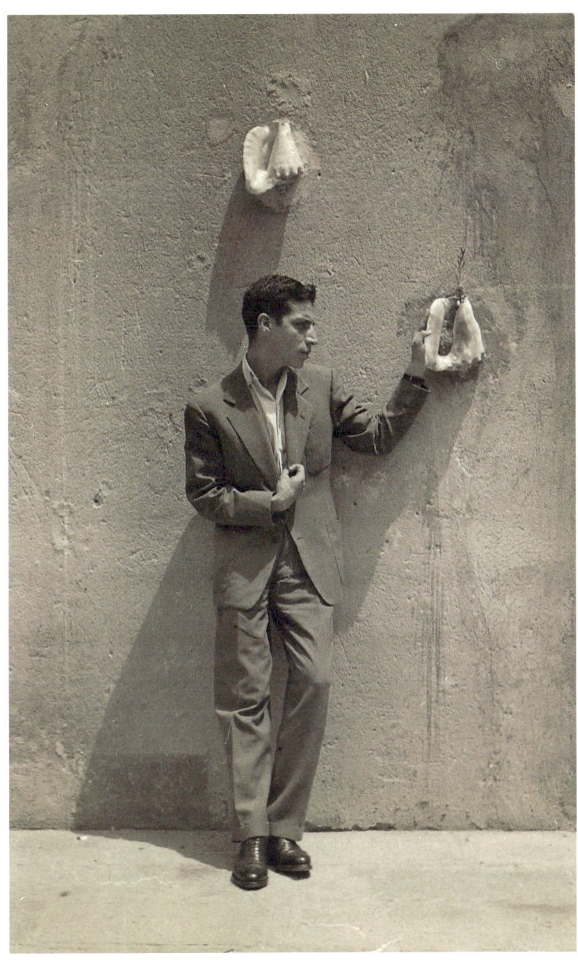

FIG. 6. Lola Alvarez Bravo. *Juan Soriano in the Patio of the Casa Azul, Mexico City*, c. 1945. Photograph, 9¼ x 5⅞ inches (23.5 x 14.9 cm). Fundación Juan Soriano y Marek Keller A.C., Mexico City. Courtesy Center for Creative Photography, University of Arizona. © 1995 The University of Arizona Foundation

and poetic, given Soriano's bawdy sense of humor it is not inconceivable that he was striking an ironic pose. The setting of this photograph is the patio of the Casa Azul, the childhood home of Frida Kahlo in the Coyoacán district of Mexico City, where she lived with her husband, Diego Rivera. Taken around 1945, at a time when Alvarez Bravo executed a number of important photographs of Kahlo, it attests to the young artist's relationship with the Mexican art world's "power couple."[37] While Soriano was not an intimate friend of Rivera (and actually disliked most of his mural paintings, along with Mexican muralism in general), they maintained cordial relations throughout the 1940s.[38] As for Kahlo, he stated:

> Frida was a victim. She had a terrible problem with her leg, but she had a tremendous personality, like a little child full of life. Later Diego came along and dressed her up in those Tehuana clothes. . . . She was a beautiful person, and she re-invented herself. Diego made her "very Mexican," but those clothes looked wonderful on her. She organized her life very well. She painted all of those pictures which I think are very beautiful.[39]

A photograph of the younger Soriano on the beach (fig. 7) is from a series of revealingly intimate, candid images captured by Alvarez Bravo during one of their numerous trips throughout Mexico with his sister Martha, her lover Rebeca Uribe, and others. ("We always had a marvelous time in those little hotels," he recalled; "I began to be seduced by nature, the trees, the sky."[40]) This example, taken in 1937 at the beach at Chachalacas, near Veracruz, suggests Soriano's constant preoccupation with sketching and drawing.

By the time this photograph was taken, Soriano had lived in the Mexican capital for two years. He was at first overwhelmed by the vastness of the metropolis, finding it "gigantic, unapproachable, and very mysterious,"[41] but accommodated to its pace and quickly made friends from virtually all social classes. His first residence was in a small apartment owned by his maternal aunt Inés. Later, his sister Martha moved to Mexico City, as did his parents and other family members, and he was able to live with them in more hospitable circumstances in an apartment on the calle Bucareli. Almost as soon as he arrived in Mexico City, Soriano became a teacher, giving art classes to working-class students at the Escuela para Obreros. One of the other teachers with whom the sixteen-year-old painter maintained a relationship was Santos Balmori. Aside from giving Soriano informal lessons, he was also influential in introducing him to an organization that played a short-lived but pivotal role in the Mexican cultural scene of the mid-1930s.

The LEAR, or Liga de Escritores y Artistas Revolucionarios, was a meeting and exhibition space, artists' and writers' collective, and organization for social action. It existed between 1934 and 1938, and its founding members included Siqueiros, the printmaker

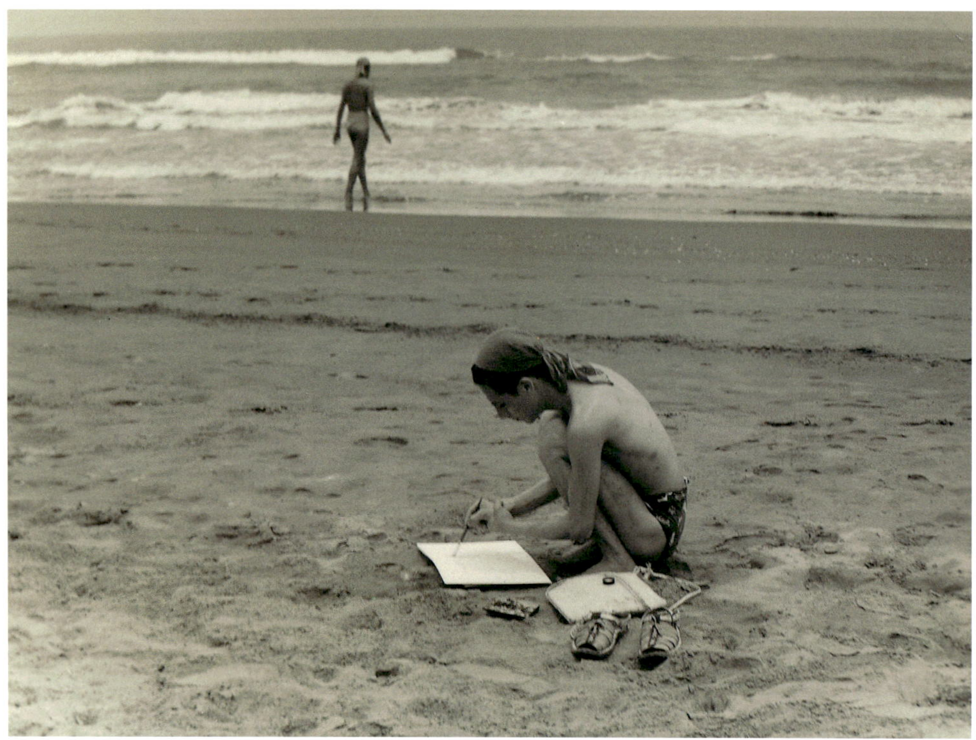

FIG. 7. Lola Alvarez Bravo. *Juan Soriano on the Beach at Chachalacas, Veracruz,* 1937. Photograph, 5⅛ x 7 inches (13 x 17.8 cm). Fundación Juan Soriano y Marek Keller A.C., Mexico City. Courtesy Center for Creative Photography, University of Arizona. © 1995 The University of Arizona Foundation

Leopoldo Méndez, the composer Silvestre Revueltas, and the Estridentista poet Germán List Arzubide. Soriano was undoubtedly interested in exhibiting with them because the membership included many of his friends from Guadalajara, such as Alvarez Bravo, Chávez Morado, Izquierdo, and Guerrero Galván. Soriano participated in one LEAR exhibition in 1936, but considered the experience a fiasco. He resigned immediately, stating that he found the organization's membership rules and social activist stance "virtually fascistic," and vowing that he would never join another group—whether artistic or political—and he never did.[42] However, the LEAR exhibition, in the deconsecrated church of Santa Clara, proved to offer more opportunities for him than he realized. A few days after the opening a major review appeared in the newspaper *Hoy*. Written by film director Chano Urueta, it extolled the talents of Soriano, stating that the young artist would "surely become one of our most representative painters." This lengthy article was accompanied by only one illustration, that of the single oil painting in the show by Soriano—*Girl with the Head of a Monkey* (fig. 8)—described as possessing "a profound, subjective beauty, an unknown esoteric attractive quality."[43] Thus despite his dismay at the exhibition of what he termed "la horrible LEAR," Soriano critically stole the show and was launched onto the Mexican art scene as a true *enfant prodigue*.[44]

Soriano said of his portraits of the 1930s that he desired to create exact depictions of the sitters, not psychologically charged images of them. He described the *Portrait of Rebeca Uribe with the Eye of Martha* (fig. 9) as an homage to the painter Mario Alonso (a favorite of the Contemporáneos), who worked "in the Oriental style, very similar to Balinese art." He also admitted a fondness for early Renaissance Florentine drawings and consciously appropriated their crisp, linear style.[45] This painting is, on all counts, a strange, enigmatic image. Rebeca Uribe and Soriano's sister lived together at the time. She is dressed in a rose-colored tunic that appears sculpted rather than

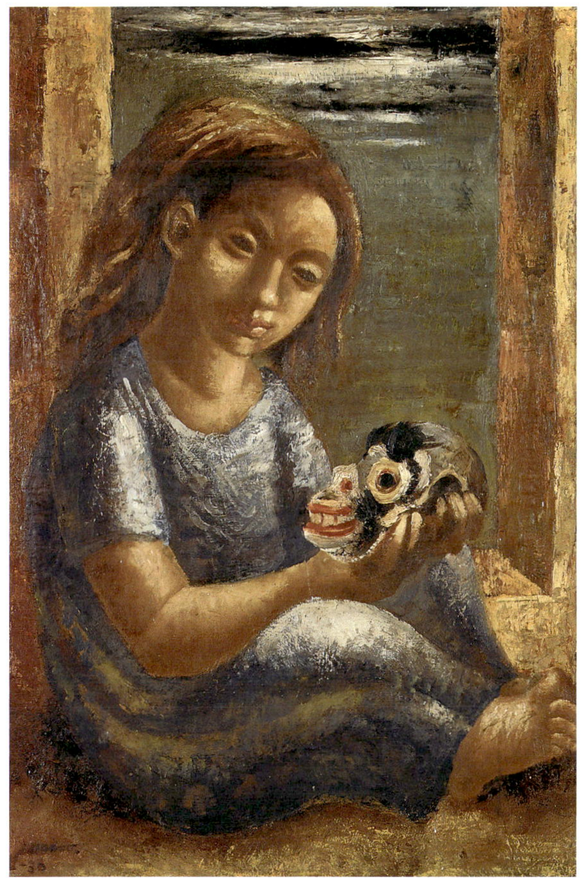

FIG. 8. *Girl with the Head of a Monkey (Girl with a Mask)*, 1936. Oil on canvas, 29⅜ x 20⅛ inches (74.5 x 51 cm). Private collection. Courtesy of the Fundación Juan Soriano y Marek Keller A.C., Mexico City

painted.[46] Spiky leaves, resembling spindly fingers, form a nettle-like background separating her from the sky. These carefully painted sinuous plant forms, adding a somewhat dream-like atmosphere to the scene, remind us of the otherworldly still lifes of Soriano's fellow painter González Serrano.[47] The sitter's features are painstakingly etched, especially her carefully plucked brows that rise high above her eyes. Her left hand protrudes from her garment and holds the form of an eye. This adds a bizarre touch to the picture and begs an explanation. Could this be a reference to an actual eye, or to the infamous scene in the then-popular 1929 Surrealist film *Un Chien Andalou* by Luis Buñuel and Salvador Dalí, in which a straight razor is used to split open a woman's eye? More likely, however, this eye is actually a painting within a painting, an example of the artistic tradition of eye portraiture. These are small, cameo-like pictures, often painted on ivory, bearing the image of the eye of a beloved, serving as a constant reminder of the part of the body known as the window to the soul. Eye portraiture, which originated in Europe in the eighteenth century (and possibly earlier), was still being practiced in Mexico in the mid-twentieth century, and it would have been logical for an intimate friend of Martha Soriano to own such an object.[48]

The *Portrait of Rebeca Uribe* also testifies to Soriano's continued interest in nineteenth-century Mexican provincial portraiture, as typified by the work of José María Estrada and others (including many anonymous artists) that he had come to know in Guadalajara. In 1943 the painter and critic Ramón Gaya underlined this affinity, remarking that "the work of Soriano is as primitive as that of Estrada. They both have the same concept of [portrait] painting. . . . They felt it to be like the veil of Veronica, quietly caressing the face."[49]

The type of highly refined, somewhat stiff, and hieratic images painted by Estrada and his contemporaries in Jalisco, Querétaro, Puebla, and elsewhere in nineteenth-century Mexico is well represented by the anonymous *Portrait of the Condesa de Canal* (fig. 10) in the Philadelphia Museum of Art. This picture offers a telling contrast to Soriano's portrait of Rebeca Uribe.[50] While obviously not a direct precedent for the 1937 work, this likeness (possibly from Guadalajara) displays an elegant woman posed against a minimal background. The noble woman in this portrait also grasps an unusual (for the time) object—a diminutive cigarette. Because nineteenth-century women usually smoked only in the privacy of their homes, this tiny element, like Martha's eye, attests to the intimate nature of the work.

The heritage of nineteenth-century Mexican portraiture is also felt in Soriano's *Portrait of Rafael Solana* of 1938 (fig. 11). Solana, a poet, novelist, and playwright who was Soriano's friend and traveling companion (in 1938 they made a trip together to San Francisco, the painter's first foreign journey), was closely associated with the Contemporáneos. Soriano stated that he found his friend (who aspired to be a bullfighter as well as a man of letters) to be "somewhat old-fashioned" and accordingly painted him in

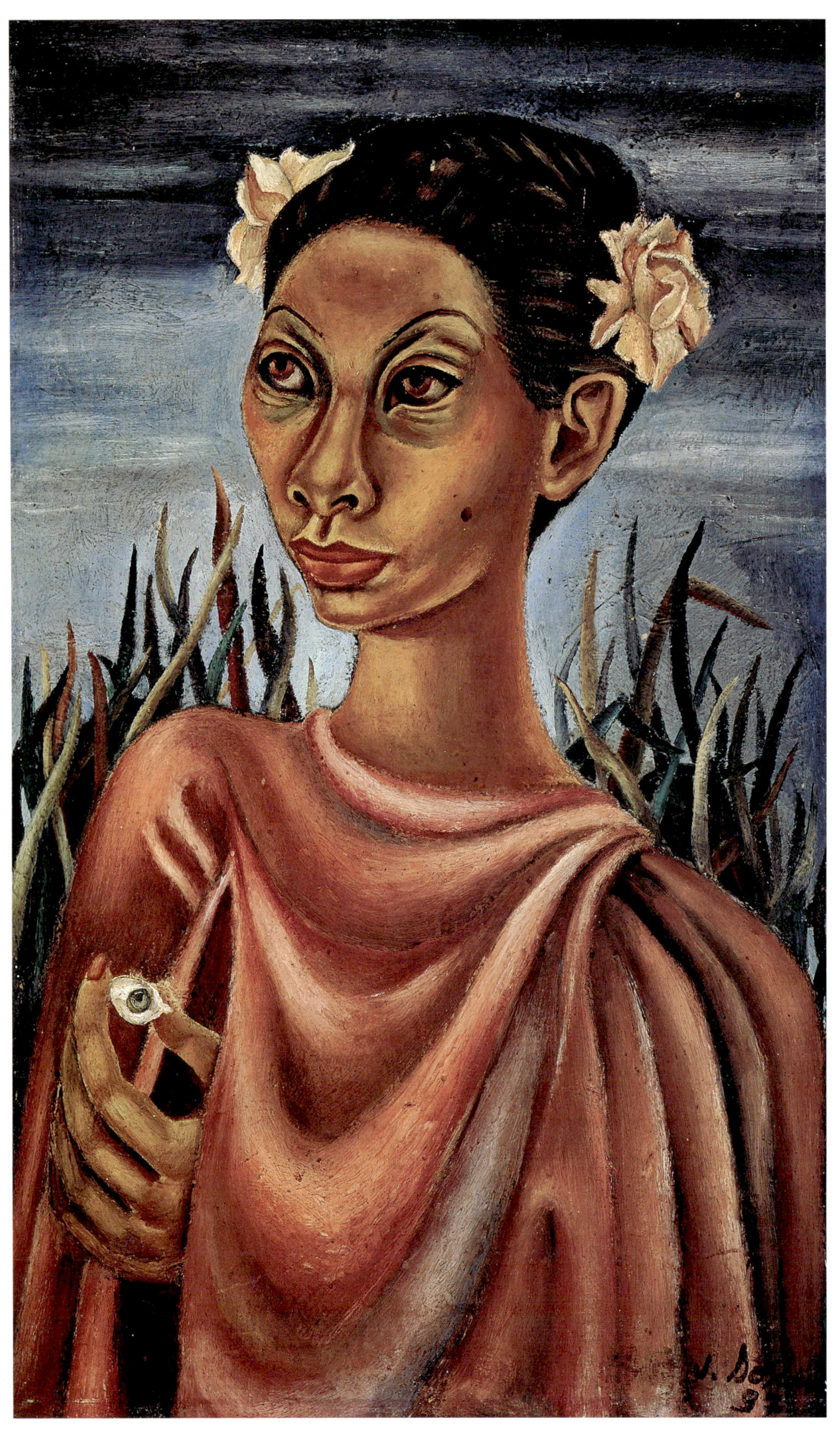

*FIG. 9. *Portrait of Rebeca Uribe with the Eye of Martha*, 1937. Oil on wood, 18⅞ x 11⅝ inches (48 x 29.5 cm). Fundación Juan Soriano y Marek Keller A.C., Mexico City

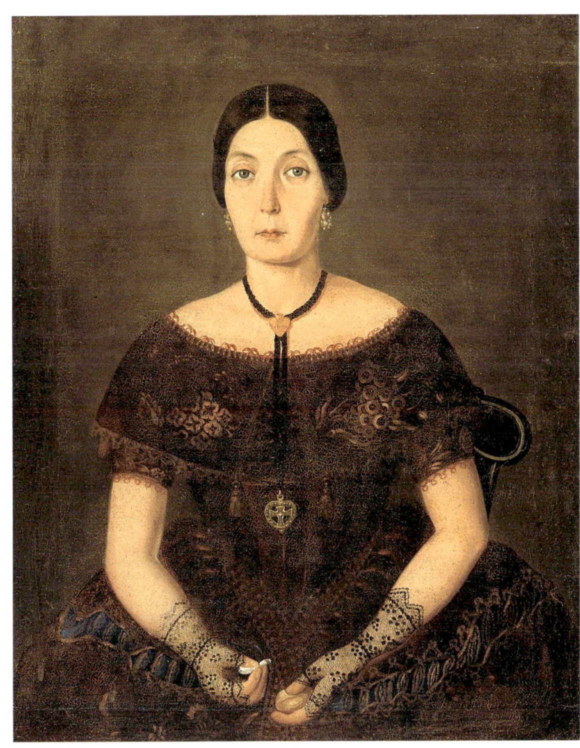

FIG. 10. Artist unknown. *Portrait of the Condesa de Canal.* Mexican, nineteenth century. Oil on canvas, $25\frac{3}{16}$ x 20 inches (64 x 50.8 cm). Philadelphia Museum of Art. Gift of Mrs. René d'Harnoncourt, 1969-273-1

an out-of-date costume.[51] The mannered portrait is placed within a highly expressive nighttime setting, which Soriano later described as being "unlike anything I had previously done."[52]

After his critical success with the LEAR exhibition in 1936, Soriano went on to participate in numerous group shows in Mexico City and elsewhere in Mexico. The notices were uniformly favorable. They consistently stressed the intensity of the work as well as its "Mexican" character (something that may have irked the artist, who professed a deep aversion to any "typical" elements in his painting). One of the more compelling reviews (both for its praise of the artist and for its own poetic style) appeared in the journal *Romance* on August 15, 1940. Written by Lorenzo Valera, it assessed the *Exposición Hispano-Mexicana* at the Librería de Cristal (one of the several bookshops in Mexico City that displayed contemporary art), in which Soriano participated along with a number of émigré painters who had fled the Spanish Civil War (a group with whom the artist had many important friendships in the 1940s). Among the Spaniards were Enrique Climent, Ramón Gaya, and Antonio Rodríguez Luna. Soriano, along with the venerable Dr. Atl (Gerardo Murillo), formed the Mexican contingent. Valera wrote:

> The pictures of Juan Soriano appear to have been painted after an excess of fever and they express an intimate condition, the very soul of the painter. It would seem then as if the painter were ill. . . . He appears . . . imprisoned within a strange personal anxiety, far from the world, lost in the most remote origins of his existence, and therefore completely distant from the gaze of others.[53]

One year later the critic José Luis Martínez described the work in Soriano's first one-artist show at the Galería Universitaria (the art gallery of the national university) as "expressing his world, speaking to us simply in an intimate Mexican voice."[54] Martínez's essay is especially interesting for its identification of the artist's principal concerns: "He does not paint, nor does he pretend to illustrate social themes, and he

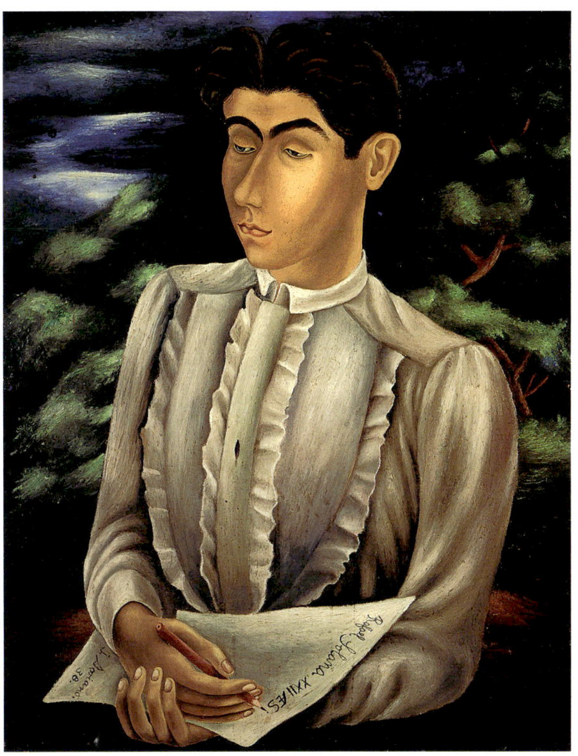

FIG. 11. *Portrait of Rafael Solana*, 1938. Oil on canvas, $30\frac{5}{16}$ x $24\frac{1}{4}$ inches (77 x 61.5 cm). Fundación Juan Soriano y Marek Keller A.C., Mexico City

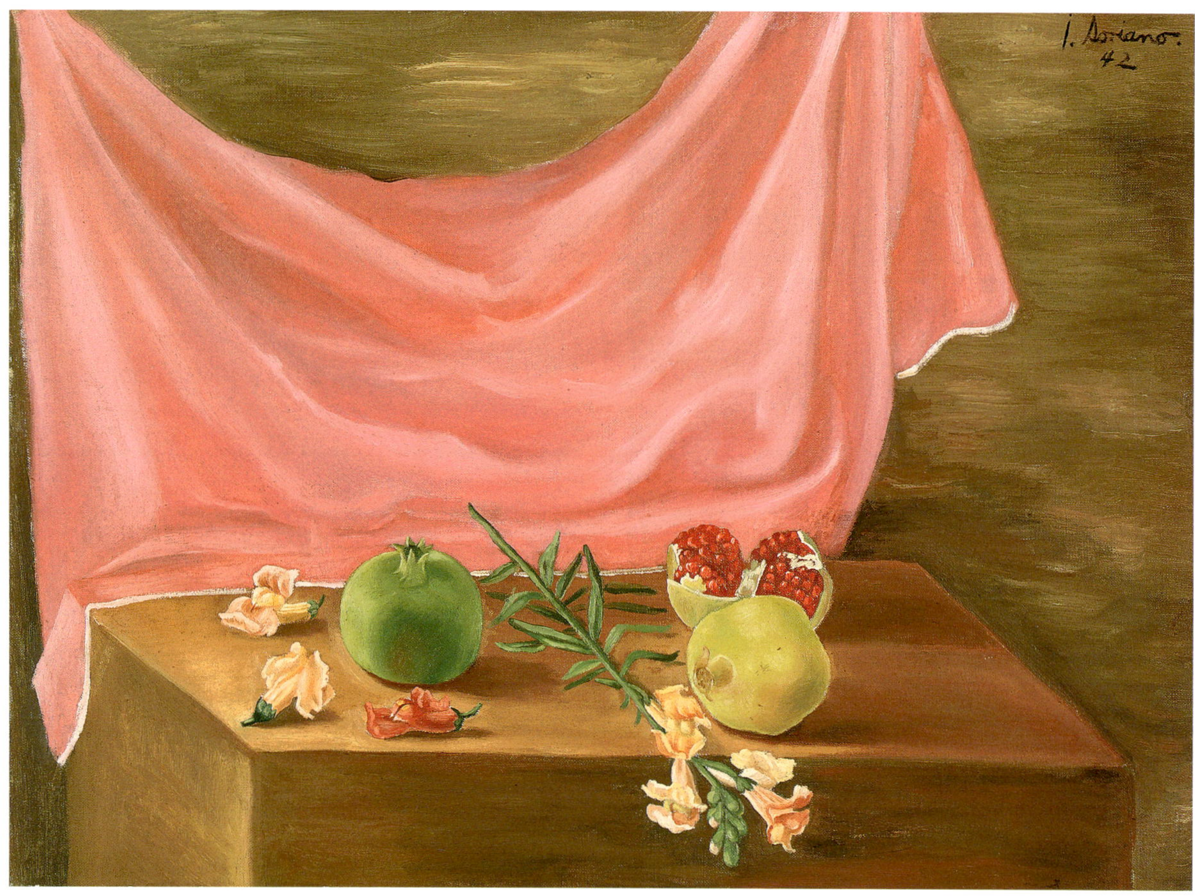

*FIG. 12. *Still Life*, 1942. Oil on canvas, 19⅝ x 27⅝ inches (49.8 x 70.2 cm). Philadelphia Museum of Art. Gift of Mr. and Mrs. Joseph J. Gersten, 1951-120-4

is not interested in drawing as a pure plastic amusement. . . . His painting evidences three themes: eroticism, religiosity, and death, whose expression comes about with the intimate sensibility of the Mexican."[55]

Although Soriano had met Inés Amor, director of the Galería de Arte Mexicano, shortly after arriving in Mexico City in 1935 (the same year Inés's sister Carolina founded the gallery), he did not have a solo show there until March 1945 (sandwiched between exhibitions in February of the Austrian Surrealist Wolfgang Paalen and in April of his fellow Guadalajara artist Raúl Anguiano, who was also working at this time in a semi-Surrealist mode).[56] Soriano's second one-artist show at Amor's gallery took place in October 1947. On November 6 of that year a review of the show by Jorge Juan Crespo de la Serna in the influential conservative daily *Excélsior* was provocatively entitled "Mundo pagano y demoníaco de Juan Soriano" (Pagan and Demonic World of Juan Soriano).[57]

Still-life paintings formed a significant component of Soriano's work during this period. The roots of his interest in still life are found in his native Jalisco and other provinces of central Mexico, where an active group of nineteenth-century still-life artists (including Agustín Arrieta and Carlos Villaseñor) had produced works that evidenced their (mostly second- or third-hand) knowledge of European (principally Dutch and Flemish) still-life painting while possessing their own disarming directness.[58] Soriano would have had ample opportunity to see such pictures in Chucho Reyes's collection in Guadalajara. In addition, these modest paintings were often found in the bourgeois homes of his childhood. Soriano's own still lifes of the late 1930s and 1940s range from direct and quietly poetic images to eerily bizarre compositions.

Two still lifes from 1942 and 1946 in the Philadelphia Museum of Art (figs. 12, 13) are appealing studies of form and color. The 1942 *Still Life* is dominated by

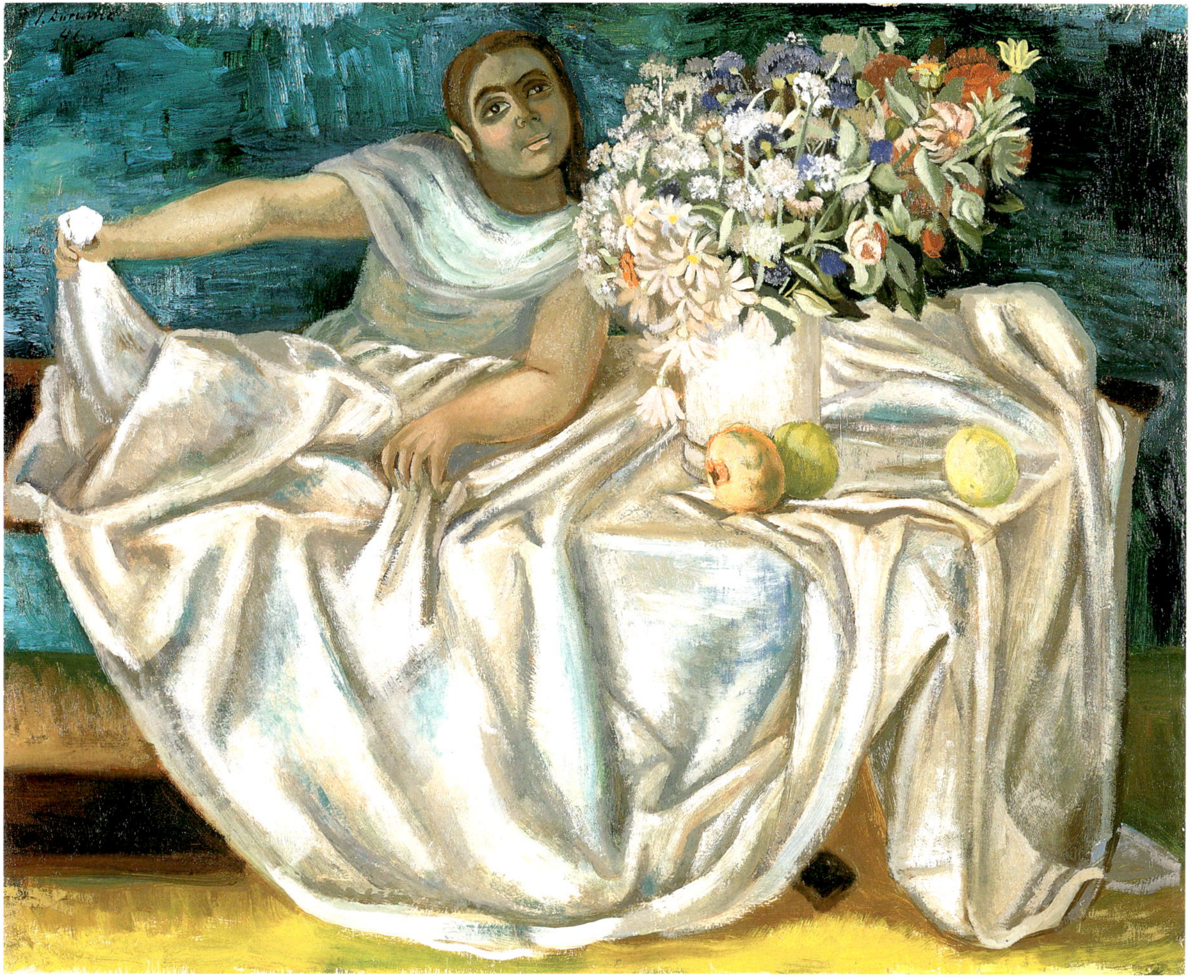

*FIG. 13. *Girl with Bouquet*, 1946. Oil on canvas, 18½ x 23¾ inches (47 x 60.3 cm). Philadelphia Museum of Art. Gift of Mr. and Mrs. Herbert Cameron Morris, 1957-94-1

pinks and reds, its lush pink cloth forming a dramatic background for the lilies, carnations, and pomegranates on the tabletop. By contrast, the 1946 *Girl with Bouquet* represents (with the exception of the blue wall behind the figure) a study in varying tones of white, from the luxurious textile draped across the table to the child's dress and the flowers in a vase. Two other striking examples evoke more questions and are more disturbing for their unusual contents. In the 1938 *Still Life with Insect* (fig. 14) a large roll of seemingly brittle, cracked paper is tipped up at an improbable angle on a black tabletop. A small group of dried flowers, a key, and a very large insect that has landed on one of the dried leaves appear to float above the scroll. Such improbable juxtapositions and the instability of the work's components enhance the disorientation experienced by the viewer. The 1941 *Still Life with Vase and Skull* (fig. 15) crosses the boundary into the realm of a dream. On a window ledge, at the left, are a glass with two marbles and a large hat pin. Bisecting the surface is a sheaf of wheat next to which is a human skull covered with a diaphanous blue-green cloth. While the presence of the skull immediately calls to mind *memento mori* iconography of traditional European still lifes, its references to death and the obvious strangeness of the juxtapositions of objects also compel us to consider the artist's relationship to Surrealism, a mode of vision, thought, and literary expression that had a complex history in Mexico City in the late 1930s and early 1940s.[59]

In another still life that offers a compelling grouping of unusual subjects, the artist places himself at

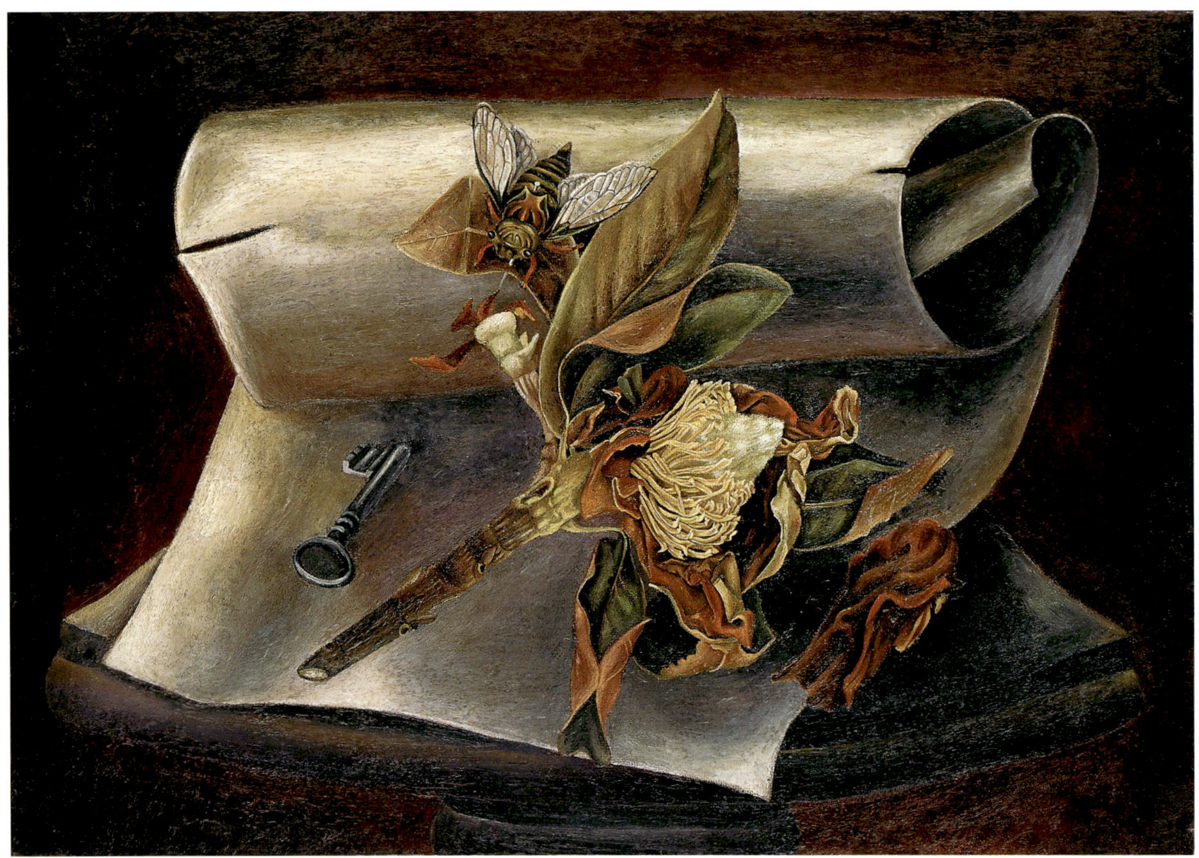

*FIG. 14. *Still Life with Insect*, 1938. Oil on Masonite, 18⅞ x 27½ inches (48 x 70 cm). Fundación Juan Soriano y Marek Keller A.C., Mexico City

the center of the composition. The 1949 *Still Life with Self-Portrait* (fig. 16) combines ears of colored corn, several glass paperweights, a small enamel sculpture of a growling Chinese dog, a bottle with a miniature scene of the crucifixion of Christ, as well as a glass beaker reflecting the artist at his easel. Soriano's interest in Northern Renaissance and Baroque painting is suggested here, and this device calls to mind similar reflections in the work of Jan van Eyck and Johannes Vermeer.

Some of Soriano's still lifes also include images of children, who play a substantial role in the artist's work of the 1940s. Soriano's children are far from the stereotypical urban working-class or rural peasant youths depicted in works by his more socially engaged contemporaries. They also exhibit little affiliation with the idealized babies or adolescents painted by colleagues such as Guerrero Galván. By contrast, Soriano's children are often unruly, misbehaving, fighting, or about to get into some other form of trouble. Take the party-dressed young blond girl in the *Untitled (Two Children)* of 1942 (fig. 17). She has just finished sliding down the long banister of a pink adobe house while a toddler (her baby brother?), wearing only a red shirt, struggles to upright himself. The girl has a slightly sinister look on her face, and the artist may be suggesting that she has just pushed the boy down the steps. The art historian Teresa del Conde noted a parallel between Soriano's paintings of adolescents and those of Balthus in their "perverse innocence."[60] While he certainly may have been familiar with Balthus's work through reproduction and may well have been influenced by it, Soriano's girls seem more seriously rebellious than the French painter's passive Lolitas.

The 1942 *Black Table* (fig. 18), another assembly of incongruously grouped elements, comprises small glass spheres, light bulbs, glass containers, a vase with

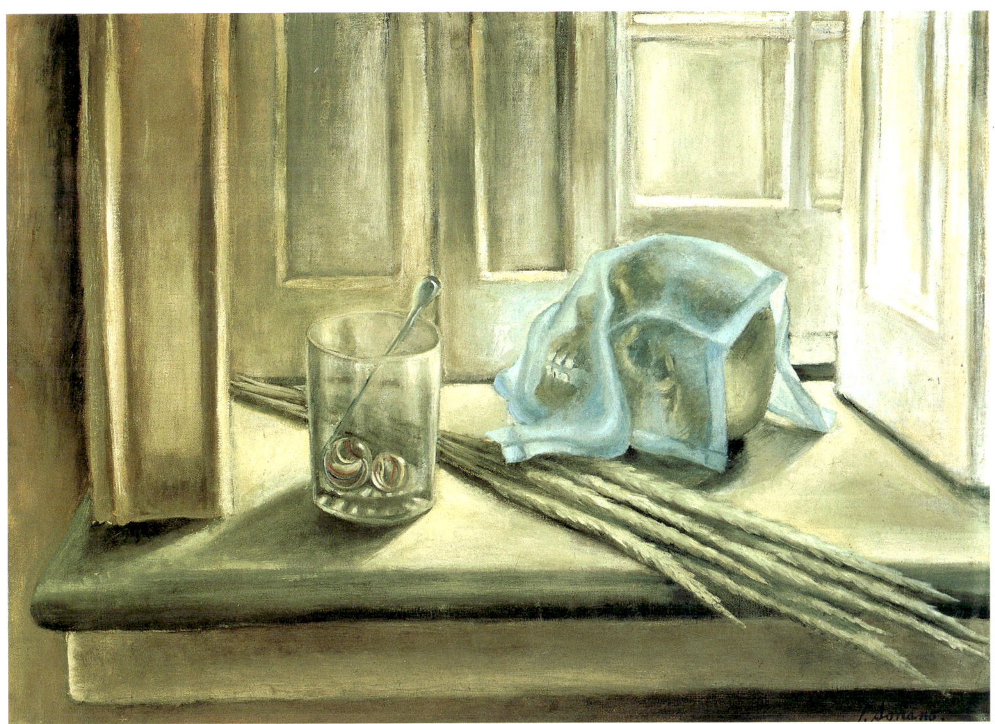

*FIG. 15. *Still Life with Vase and Skull*, 1941. Oil on canvas, 23⅝ x 31½ inches (60 x 80 cm). Fundación Juan Soriano y Marek Keller A.C., Mexico City

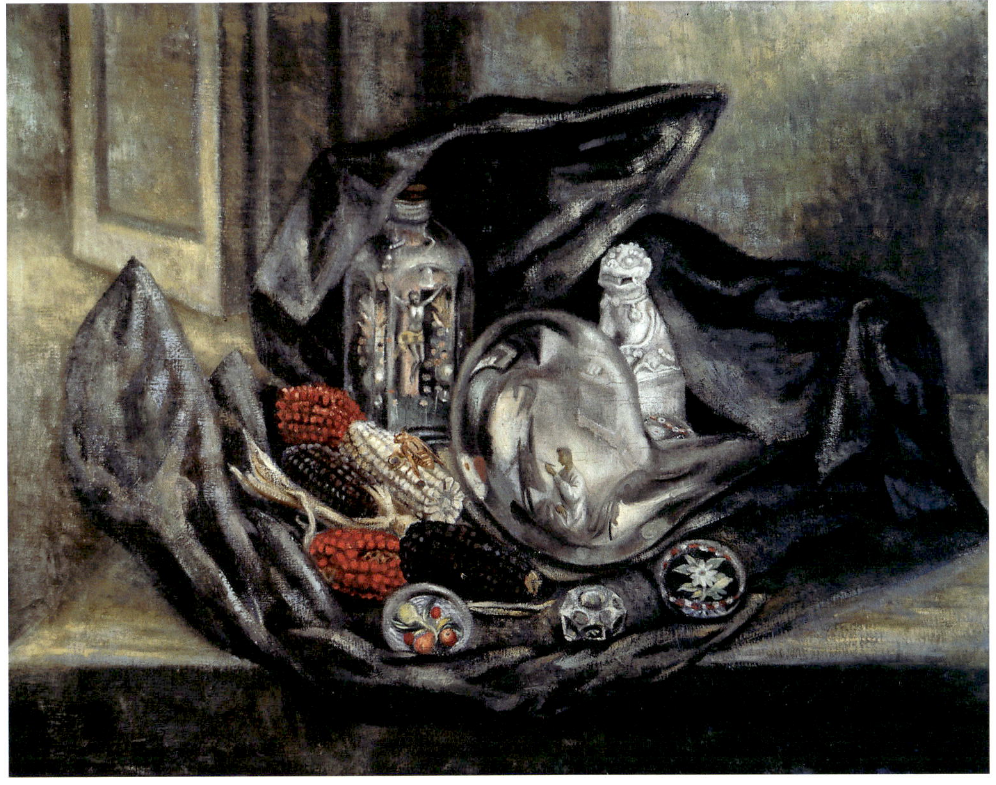

*FIG. 16. *Still Life with Self-Portrait*, 1949. Oil on canvas, 26⅛ x 31½ inches (66.5 x 80 cm). Fundación Juan Soriano y Marek Keller A.C., Mexico City

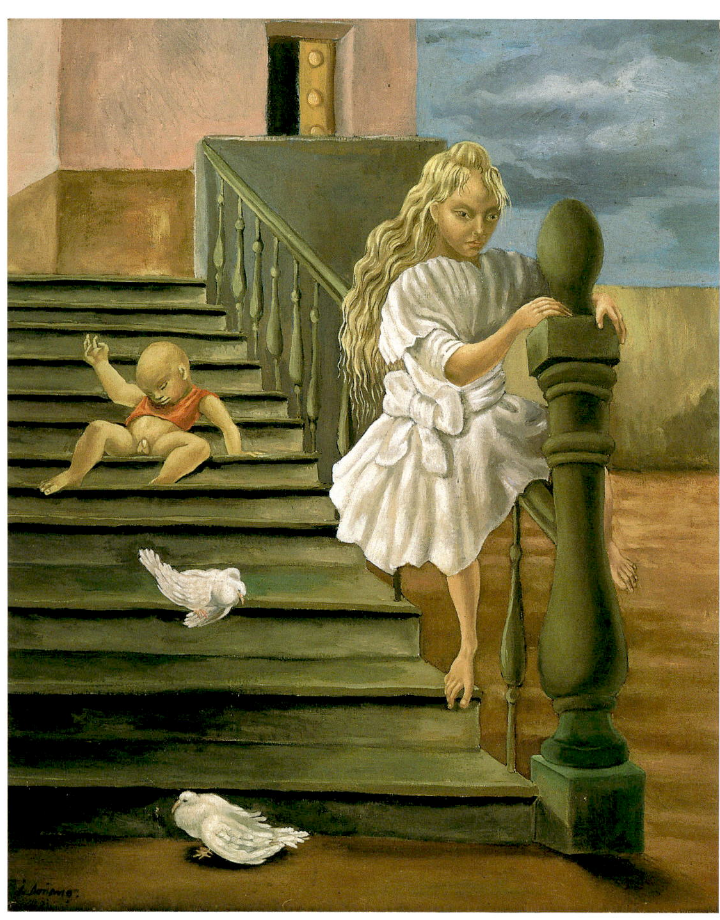

FIG. 17. *Untitled (Two Children)*, 1942. Oil on canvas, 39⅜ x 31½ inches (100 x 80 cm). Private collection. Courtesy of the Fundación Juan Soriano y Marek Keller A.C., Mexico City

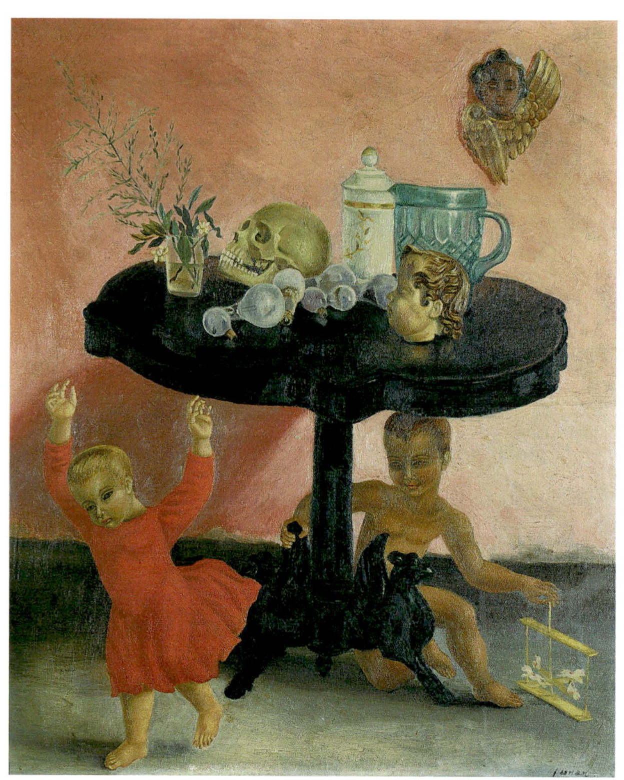

FIG. 18. *The Black Table*, 1942. Oil on canvas, 25⅝ x 21⅝ inches (65 x 55 cm). Private collection. Courtesy of the Fundación Juan Soriano y Marek Keller A.C., Mexico City

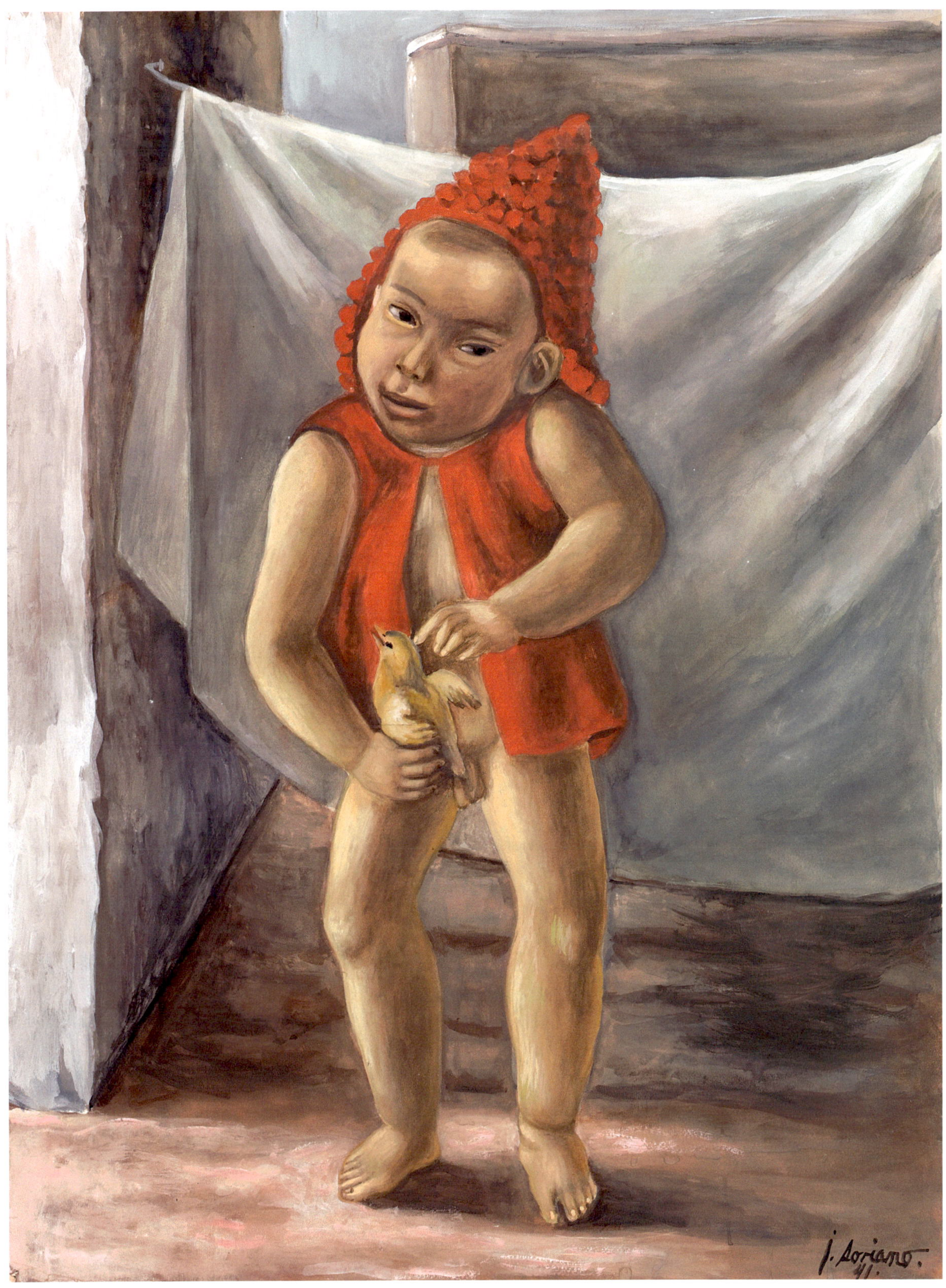

*FIG. 19. *Child with Bird*, 1941. Gouache on paper, 25½ x 19⅝ inches (64.8 x 49.8 cm). The Museum of Modern Art, New York. Inter-American Fund, 792.1942

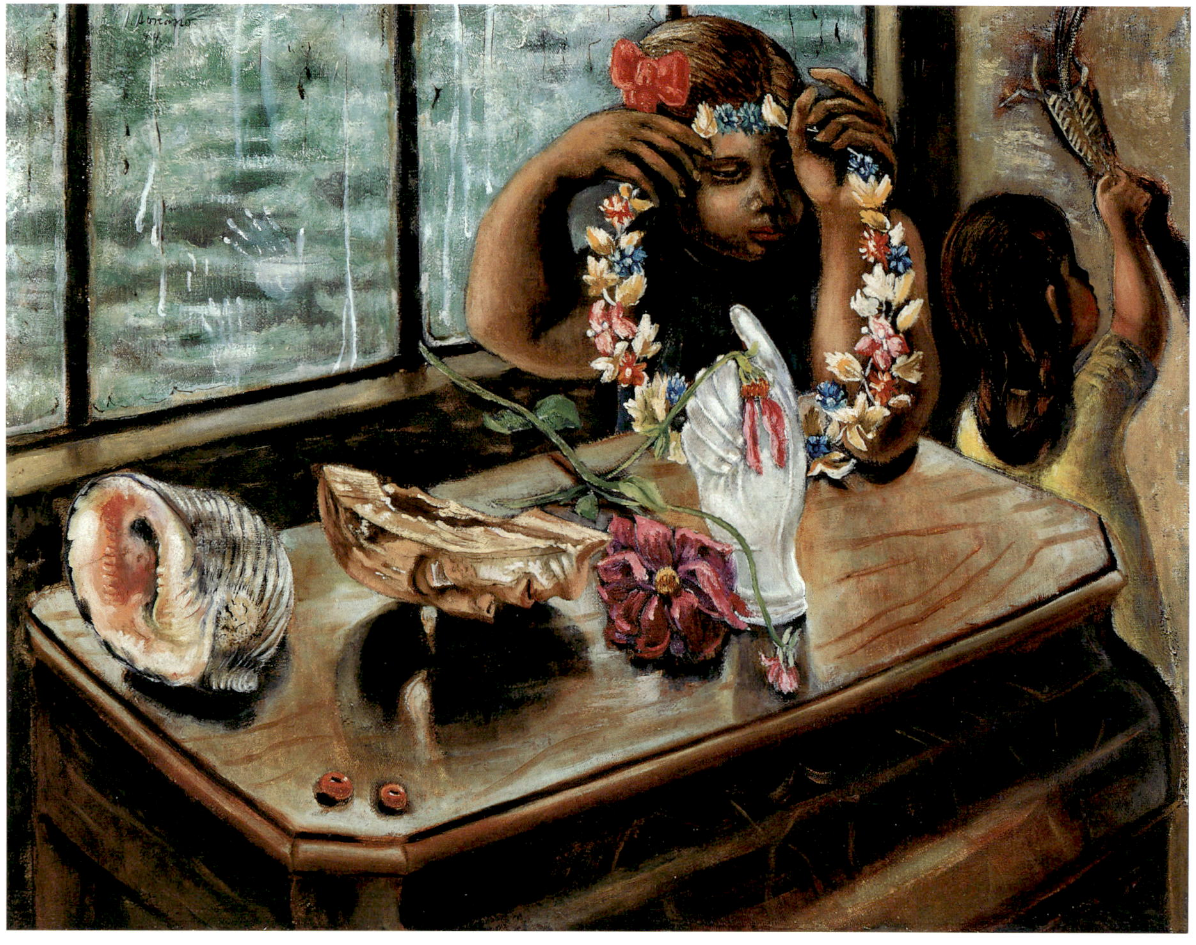

FIG. 20. *Children Playing*, 1944. Oil on canvas, 17¾ x 23⅝ inches (45 x 60 cm). Museo Andrés Blaisten, Mexico City

flowers, the broken head of a colonial statue, and a human skull. Despite the attractions of these objects, the children located below the table (the girl dressed in red, the slightly older boy naked) hold our gaze more directly. The scowling little girl runs away from the boy, who grasps a small wooden toy. He has obviously frightened her in their sinister game of hide-and-seek.

The 1941 gouache *Child with Bird* (fig. 19) depicts an even more mischievous youth. This somewhat disconcerting image portrays a two- or three-year-old boy standing before a white sheet, as if on display in a (perverse) pantomime. The theatrical aura of the scene is enhanced by his red jacket and odd, conical cap. The boy, nude except for these garments, displays a slight smirk on his face as he grabs the small bird with his right hand, pointing to it with his left. The bird is placed directly in front of his penis. As the slang expression in Spanish for the male genitals derives from a variant of the word for "bird," it becomes obvious that this image portrays a reference to precocious sexual activity.

More enigmatic still is the dreamily lyrical *Children Playing* of 1944 (fig. 20), in which two girls appear to be adorning the wall behind them for some festive or religious event. The bulk of the space is taken up by the large tabletop, which features a conch shell, the overturned face of a plaster cast, flowers, and a strange white enamel hand with one raised finger pointing ominously to something outside the picture. The eeriness of this composition is enhanced by the effects of the rain on the window. Two handprints are seen on the glass, and, if we look closely, there appears to be the ghostly profile of a person outlined against the sky. While it may not necessarily be labeled as a Surrealist composition, this appealingly anxiety-filled can-

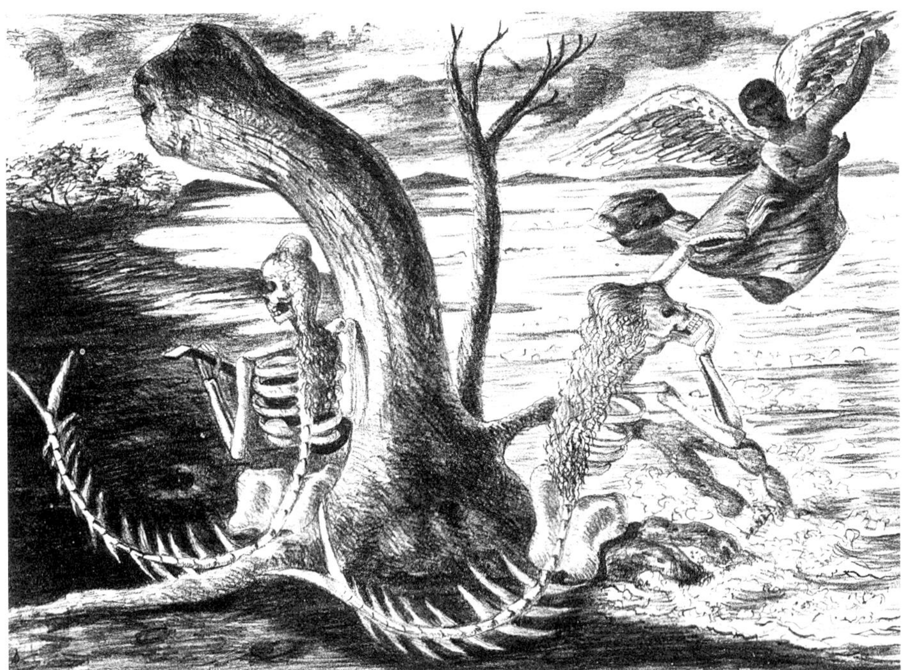

FIG. 21. *Untitled (Mermaid Skeletons)*, 1944. Lithograph, 12⅝ x 18⅞ inches (32 x 48 cm). Private collection. Courtesy of the Fundación Juan Soriano y Marek Keller A.C., Mexico City

vas certainly makes a bow in the direction of dream-related realism, which would play an increasingly important role in Soriano's art of the 1940s.

Surrealism in a Time of War

When asked if he thought there was a direct relationship between his work of this period and Surrealism, Soriano emphatically stated: "Absolutely not! My work then had nothing to do with it, and I had little interest in the self-indulgence of the so-called Surrealist artists."[61] Yet the vehemence of his reply is telling in itself, indicating that he was struggling with the concepts promoted by such gurus of Surrealism as André Breton (who came to Mexico in 1938), Wolfgang Paalen, the Peruvian poet-artist César Moro, and even Diego Rivera, all of whom were instrumental in organizing the international Surrealist exhibition that opened at the Galería de Arte Mexicano on January 17, 1940, with Juan Soriano in attendance, although his work was not included.[62]

The artist recounted to Elena Poniatowska his dismay at the pretentiousness of the opening, where all invitees were obliged to come in formal dress. At the end of the evening Soriano was so disgusted that he gave his tuxedo to a waiter, leaving with only his overcoat covering his underwear.[63] Yet, despite the artist's own dismissiveness of the movement, certain examples of his work may be connected to Surrealism, which undoubtedly formed a significant element within the Mexican art world in the late 1930s and 1940s.[64] Soriano developed friendships or acquaintanceships with some of the émigré Surrealists such as Leonora Carrington and Antonin Artaud, whom he met at the home of María Izquierdo. Yet his was not a formal affiliation with the work of these foreigners, nor a falling in line with the adaptations that some of his fellow Mexican artists (such as Guillermo Meza, Chávez Morado, or Lazo) had made to Surrealism, but rather a parallel cultivation of nonquotidian subject matter that placed Soriano, correctly or not, within the Surrealist aura. Indeed, themes that could be called Surrealist were developing in his art well before his contact with the movements or artists in the circle of Breton. The fantastical angels or skeletons, for example, that we observe in some of his paintings and prints had already interested him in his early youth in Guadalajara, when he saw them in the collection of Chucho Reyes

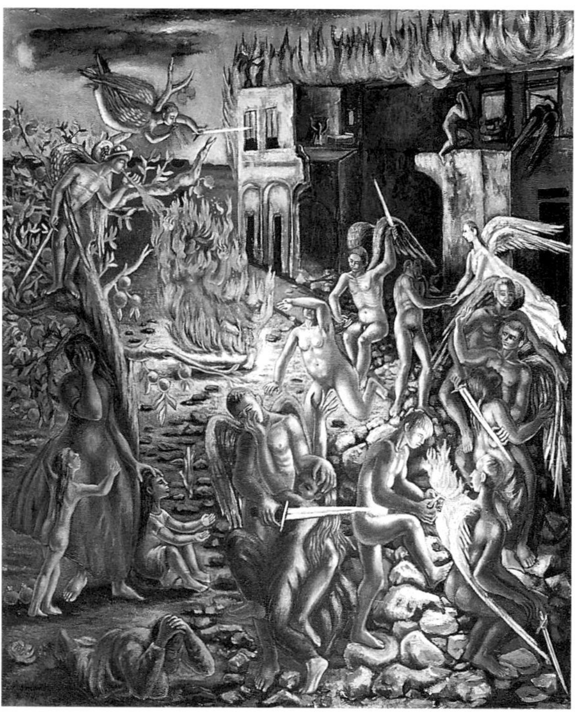

FIG. 22. *Massacre of the Innocents*, 1944. Oil on canvas, 27½ x 23⅝ inches (70 x 60 cm). Private collection. Courtesy of the Fundación Juan Soriano y Marek Keller A.C., Mexico City

(who himself painted such figures). Critics linked Soriano to Surrealism as early as the mid-1940s. A writer for *Art News*, reviewing the *Mexican Painting* exhibition at New York's Knoedler Gallery in November 1945, stated that the artist "combines the power of the older social crusaders with a disturbing, often surreal imagery."[65] Soriano continues to be included in more recent discussions of "Mexican Surrealism,"[66] and by examining a few examples of work that may be interpreted in this way we may assess his alleged affinities with the movement.

A lithograph from 1944, *Untitled (Mermaid Skeletons)* (fig. 21), features some of these unusual elements. On either side of a dead, phallic tree sit lively skeletons of mermaids, their long tails composed of a series of spiky bones and their once-luxurious hair now reduced to a tangled mess of brittle strands. The one at the left plays a guitar or lute, while her companion observes, with her hand on a bony chin, a youthful angel flying in the sky at right, gesturing upward. There is a gloomy aspect to the landscape; trees are devoid of leaves, and the sea seems about to envelope the dry land. The art historian James Oles has written an illuminating account of Rufino Tamayo's Surrealist-related wartime imagery, noting that his "easel paintings of the 1940s reveal a subtle and metaphoric meditation on the tragic events."[67] While Soriano did not express himself with the type of semi-programmatic imagery of howling dogs, vicious birds, or screaming children utilized by his friend Tamayo, he did insert subtle but no less potent hints of his anxiety at the time through the use of images such as those seen in this print, as well as other disturbing visions such as confrontations with devils or fighting animals.

Painted in the same year as the print of mermaid skeletons is the canvas known as *Massacre of the Innocents* (fig. 22). While conventional representations of this biblical episode from the infancy of Christ show the deaths of male children at the hands of King Herod's soldiers, this painting is a scene of mayhem, more akin to apocalyptic imagery. A weeping mother and child at the left witness the terror of a battle between avenging angels and hapless humans who are slaughtered with long, pointed swords. A fortress-like building in the background has been set ablaze, and the ground is littered with the dead and dying. The significance of this enigmatic scene of devastation is left to the viewer.

All three of Soriano's favorite themes of religion, eroticism, and death are present in the 1942 *Saint Jerome* (fig. 23). Borrowing and radically transforming the ancient iconography of the meditative scholar-saint surrounded by books, Soriano creates an image of male beauty at the height of perfection. The young man displays his body in a most revealing pose, becoming a virtual still life himself—an object of erotic desire. This carnal idyll is interrupted, however, by the presence of death in the form of a skeleton holding an hourglass that appears in a mirror behind the man. The skeleton's pose is virtually the same as that of the youth and thus constitutes a commentary on the ephemeral nature of life, but, more to the point, the transitory nature of physical attraction. Soriano's model for this painting was Diego de Mesa, the Spanish émigré author and socialite who became Soriano's lover and companion in Mexico and later when they lived in Europe. He is also the subject of one of the painter's most beautiful likenesses of this period, *Por-*

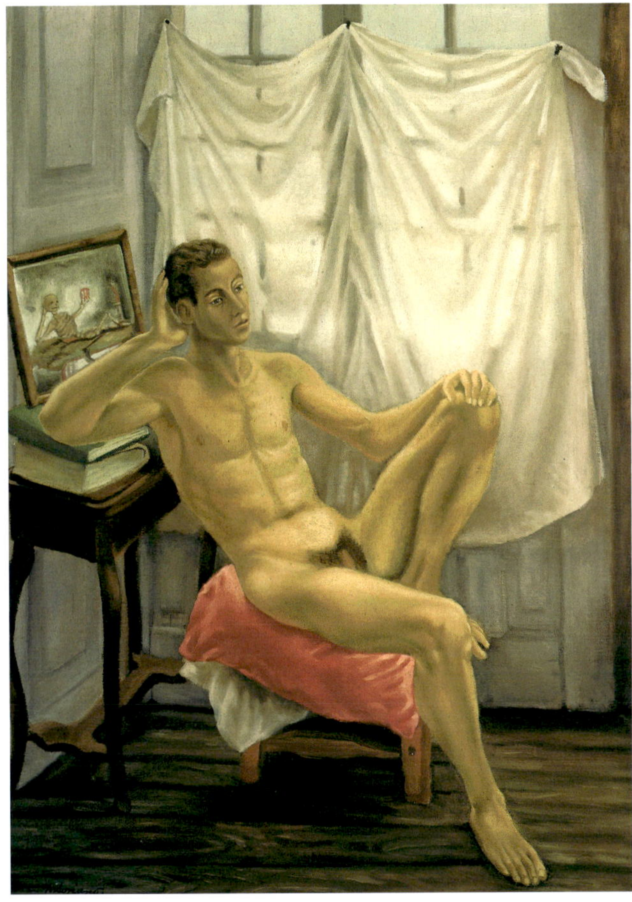

*FIG. 23. *Saint Jerome*, 1942. Oil on canvas, 31⅛ x 23¼ inches (79 x 59 cm). Fundación Juan Soriano y Marek Keller A.C., Mexico City

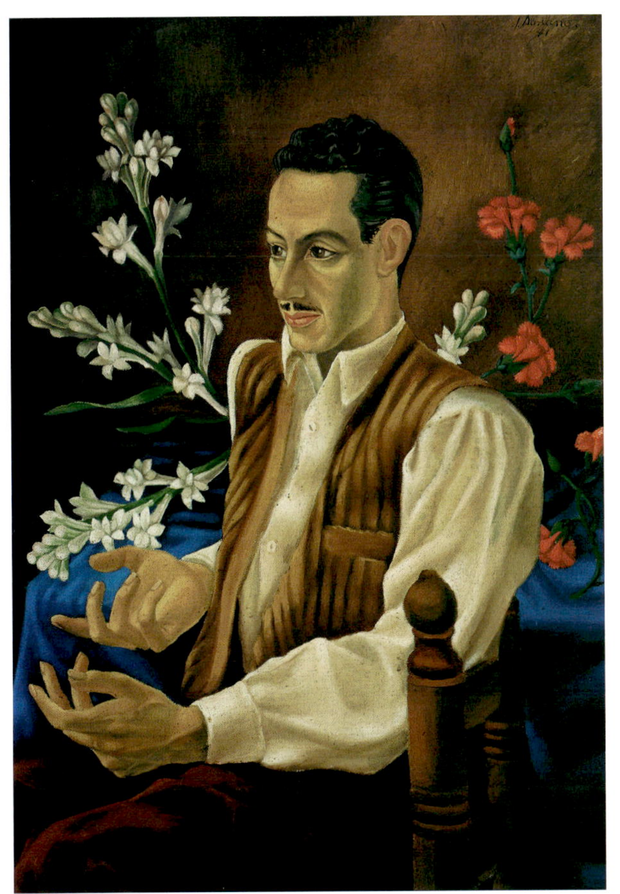

*FIG. 24. *Portrait of Diego de Mesa*, 1941. Oil on canvas, 27½ x 19$^{11}/_{16}$ inches (70 x 50 cm). Fundación Juan Soriano y Marek Keller A.C., Mexico City

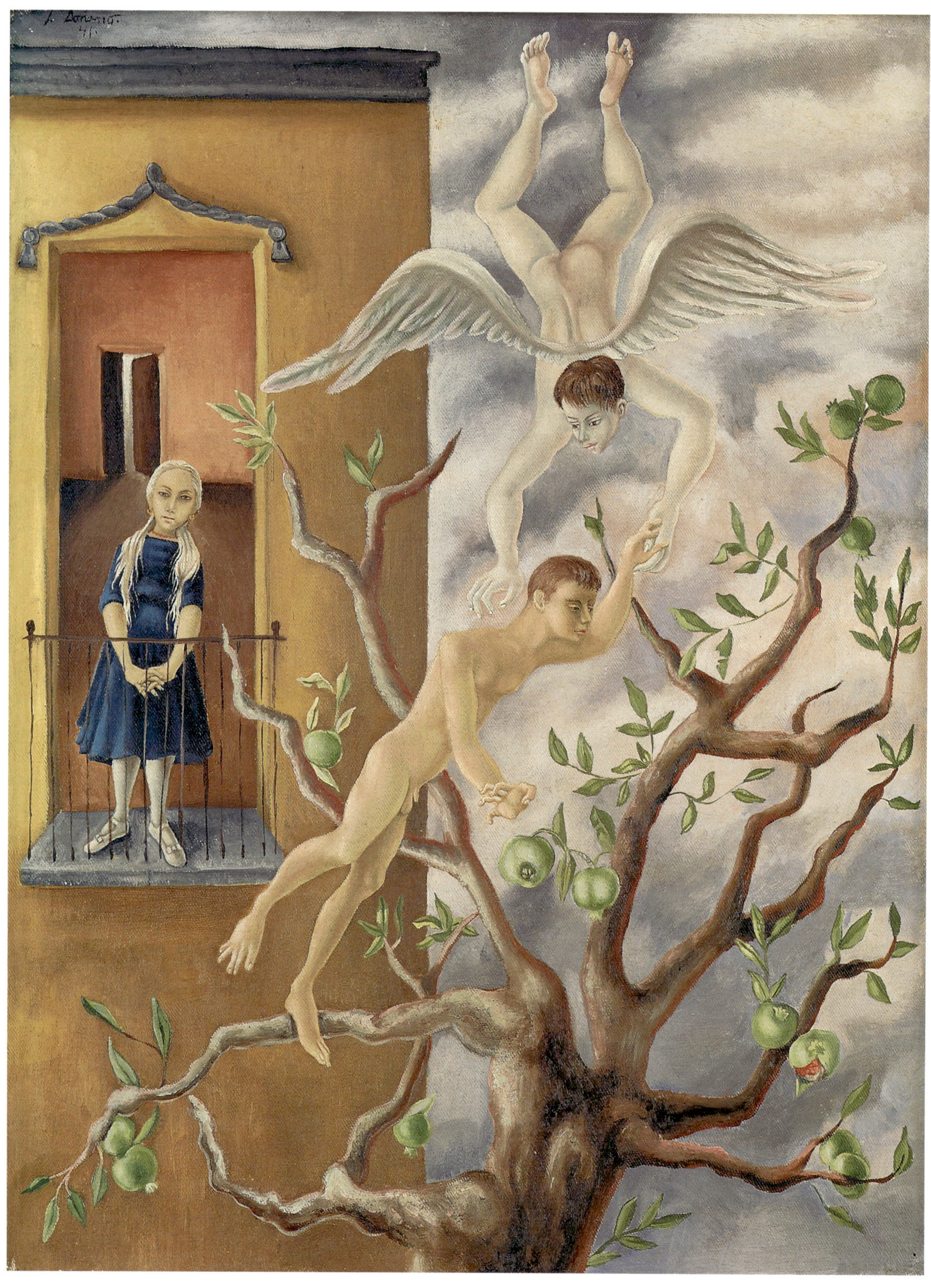

*FIG. 25. *Guardian Angel*, 1941. Oil on canvas, 23⅜ x 17¾ inches (59.5 x 45 cm). Fundación Juan Soriano y Marek Keller A.C., Mexico City

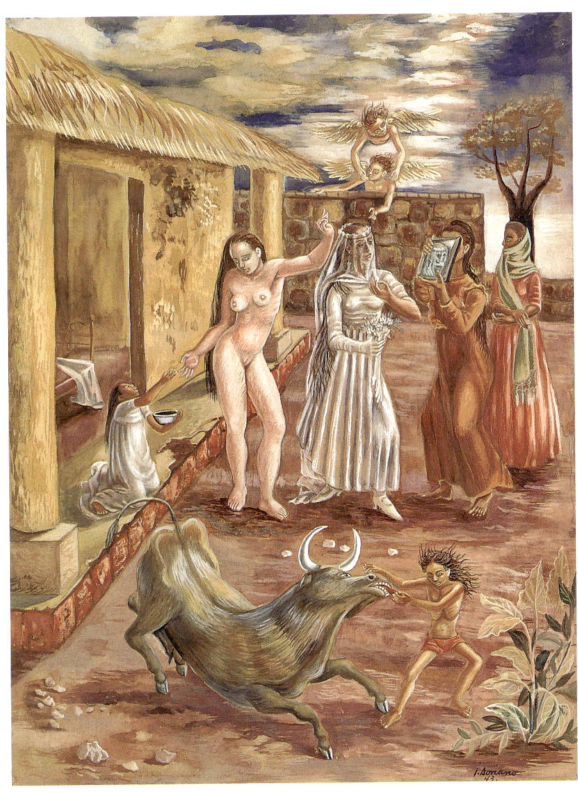

FIG. 26. *The Bartered Bride*, 1943. Gouache on paper, 25⅝ x 20¹⁄₁₆ inches (65 x 51 cm). Private collection. Courtesy of the Fundación Juan Soriano y Marek Keller A.C., Mexico City

trait of Diego de Mesa of 1941 (fig. 24), which shows the subject surrounded by carnations and tuberoses, flowers with which the artist sought to evoke Mesa's native country.

The *Saint Jerome* is one of several paintings of this period that present a voluptuous, nonaggressive view of homoerotic desire perceived through the veil of unusual or slightly disorienting circumstances. Another is the *Guardian Angel* of 1941 (fig. 25), a deliciously ambiguous composition in which a young girl is framed by the door of a balcony. She looks away from the action as a nude young man (her lover?) hurtles to earth before a tree bearing ripe pomegranates (a symbol of love and fecundity). This adolescent is aided midway in his fall by an angel, an equally handsome youth, whose skin and wings are white, in contrast to the darker complexion of the mortal he is saving from death through his seraphic touch.

The Bartered Bride (fig. 26) of 1943, one of many gouaches done during the 1940s, is perhaps one of Soriano's most inscrutable paintings. The artist stated that it was suggested by his reading of Federico García Lorca's play *Bodas de sangre* (Blood Wedding), a tale of sexual jealousy and repression set in a small town in southern Spain.[68] The scene takes place in a patio before a modest, thatched-roof house where a veiled bride is accompanied by three women. One of them holds before her a mirror offering a reflection of the bride's face transformed into a skull. Other elements of this strange drama include a kneeling girl at left holding a bowl, a pair of cherubic angels observing the scene from the wall of the patio, and a small, half-naked girl fighting a bull in the lower portion of the picture, included here, said Soriano, "simply to fill up the space."[69]

Perhaps the painting that can be most closely associated both with what the art historian Ida Rodríguez Prampolini termed the "saturated Surrealist air" of Mexico City in the 1940s[70] as well as evocations of the atmosphere during the war years is *The Beach* of 1943 (fig. 27), one of the artist's largest compositions from this time. This theatrical scene portrays a band of exhausted, desperate people, all nude, stranded on a beach observing a band of angels flying in the blood-red sky. An archangel perches on a tiny outcropping of rock in the turbulent sea just offshore. The devil has invaded their midst and embraces one of their group at the water's edge. This is, in fact, a portrait of members of Soriano's family and many of his friends.[71] In an often-quoted explanation of this painting, Soriano says that he created it to reflect his alarm at the dissolute state of his coterie in Mexico City, who "seemed ignorant of the horrible state of the world during the war and thought of nothing but pleasure and parties."[72]

The Beach is one of a number of ambitious allegorical compositions Soriano made in the 1940s. Its panoramic scope, crowded, multiplaned spatial shifts, devils and skeletons, and emphasis on linear drawing recall analogous works by other Mexican painters of the time with whom Soriano maintained relations. One particularly striking example is an ambitious canvas in the Philadelphia Museum of Art, Federico Cantú's *Triumph of Death* of 1938 (fig. 28), which MacKinley Helm gave to the Museum the year *The Beach* was painted.[73] Cantú (1907–1989), a native of the northeastern state of Nuevo León, emerged from the Open-Air School tradition in the 1920s and prac-

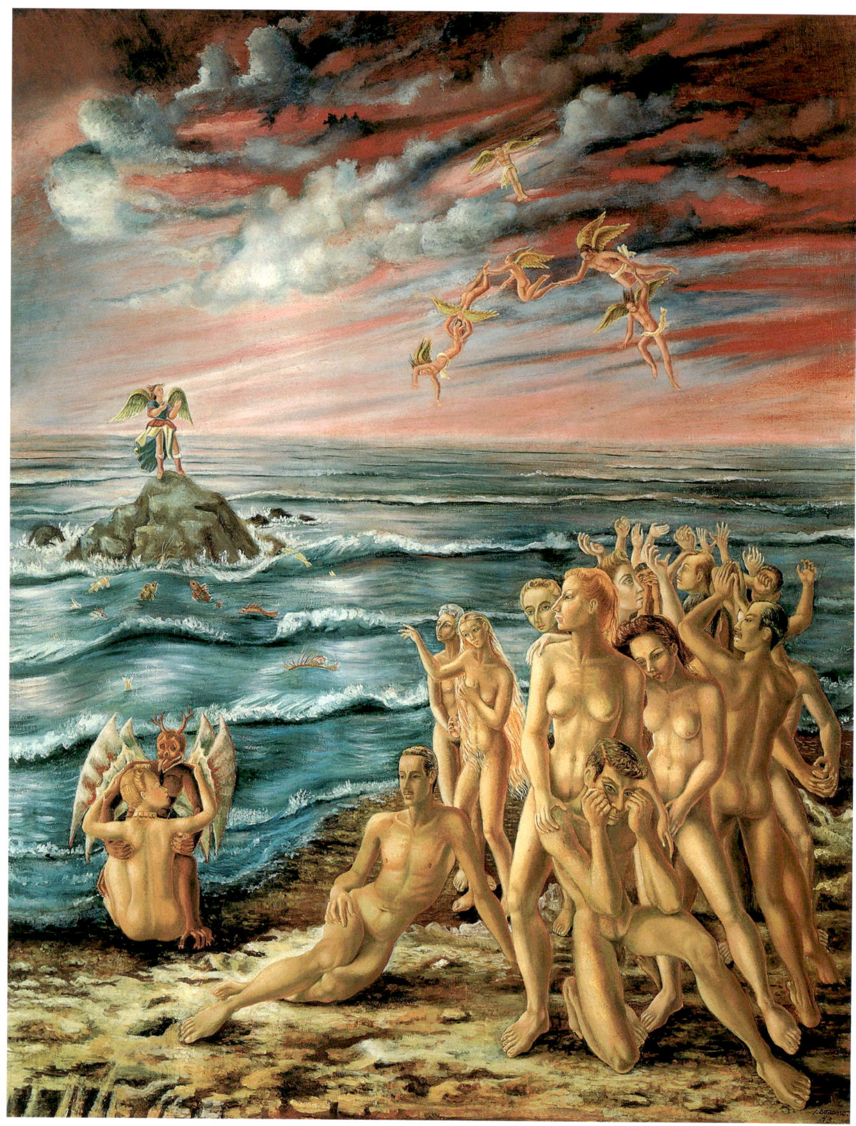

FIG. 27. *The Beach*, 1943. Oil and tempera on Masonite, 59⅞ x 48 inches (152 x 122 cm). Private collection. Courtesy of the Fundación Juan Soriano y Marek Keller A.C., Mexico City

ticed a much-admired form of detailed, academic drawing in his paintings, murals, and prints. The stylistic affinities between Soriano and Cantú have been noted by several critics.[74] Cantú's allegory includes a skeleton, a devil (observing the penitent Magdalene in a cave in the background), a musical Pierrot, and, at the highest point in the center of the composition, the artist himself viewing the proceedings. Cantú's work is as broad in its scope as *The Beach* and as redolent of despair, although by no means as clearly organized as the younger painter's composition.

Soriano himself did a number of other ambitious allegorical pictures in which he commented on the state of the world in the 1940s: *New Paradise: The Little Horses (Los Caballitos)* of 1945 (fig. 29) is a metaphor for the promise of youth as represented by the numerous children on an amusement-park ride. It has been described by the critic Justino Fernández as representing "a carnival of life."[75] In this complex picture, which evidences Soriano's long-standing interest in theatricality (the upper portion shows a stage curtain that appears to have just been lifted to reveal the scene), the artist himself is seen at the right, crouching on a plinth, with an olive-crowned, classically draped

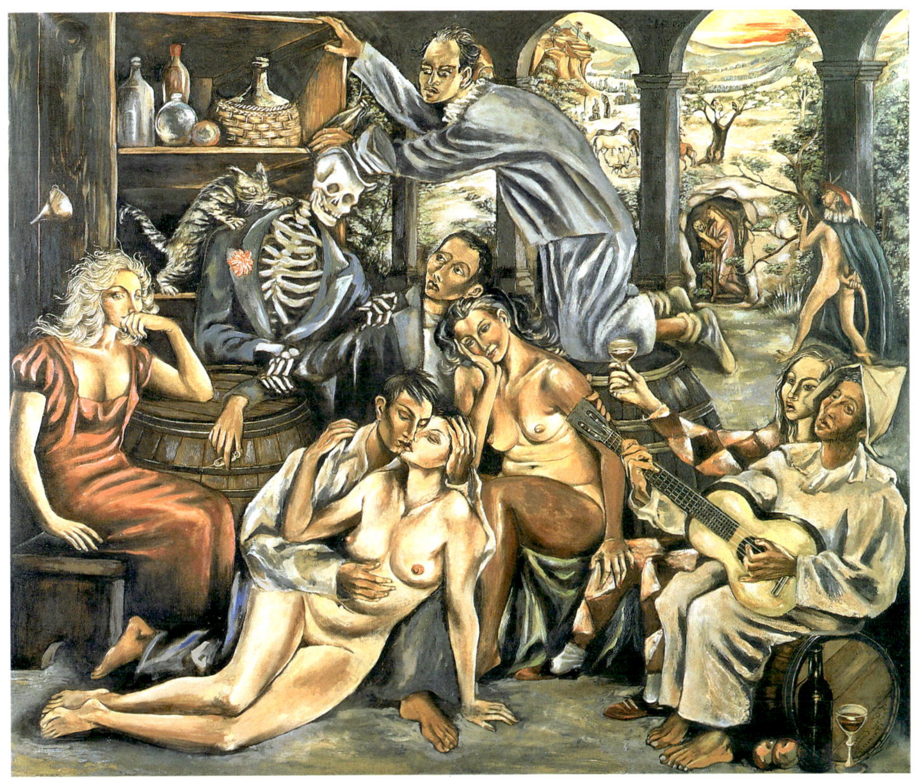

FIG. 28. Federico Cantú (Mexican, 1908–1989). *Triumph of Death*, 1938. Oil on canvas, 58¼ x 72⅝ inches (148 x 184.5 cm). Philadelphia Museum of Art. Gift of Dr. and Mrs. MacKinley Helm, 1943-44-1

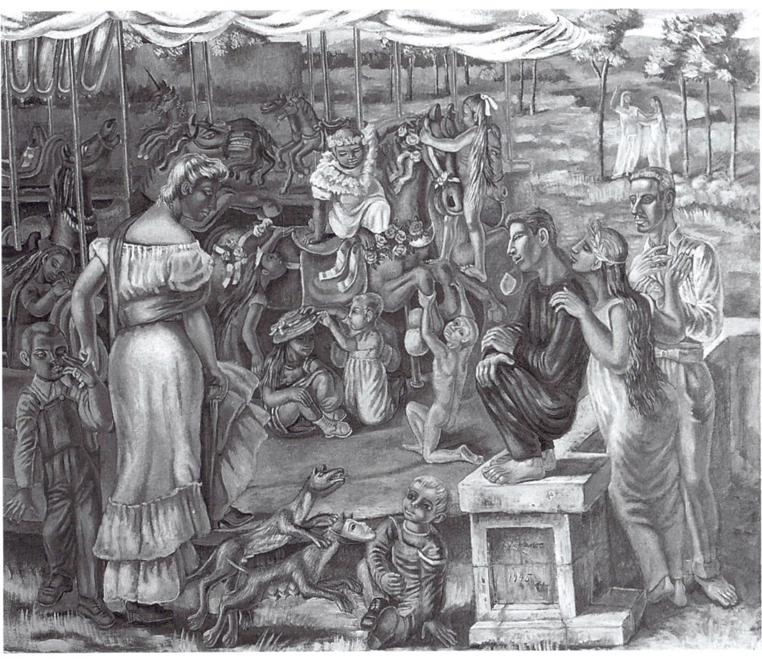

FIG. 29. *New Paradise: The Little Horses (Los Caballitos)*, 1945. Oil on canvas, 47⅝ x 59 inches (121 x 150 cm). Universidad Nacional Autónoma de México, Mexico City. Courtesy of the Fundación Juan Soriano y Marek Keller A.C., Mexico City

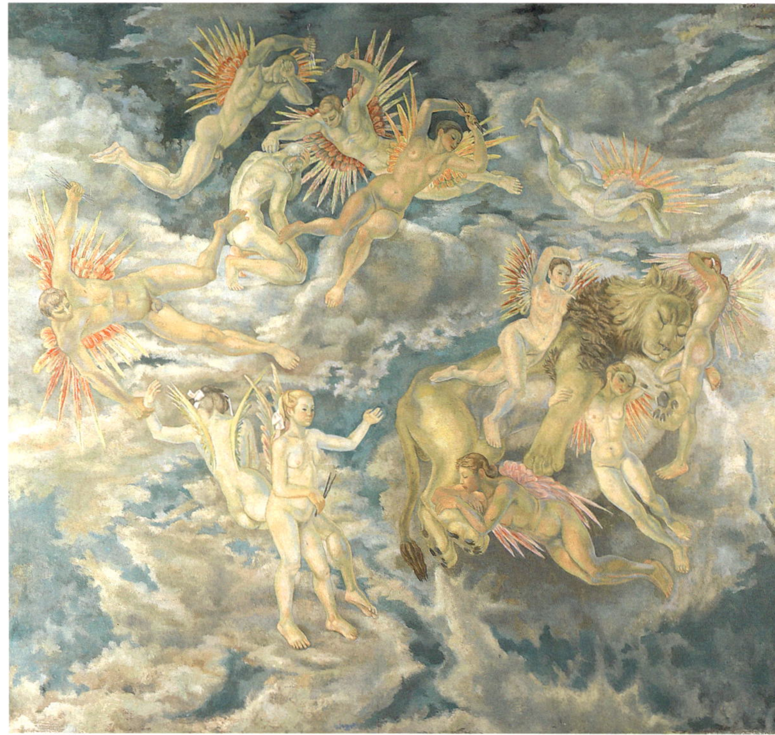

FIG. 30. *Saint Jerome Mourned by Angels*, 1949. Oil on canvas, 78¾ x 93¾ inches (200 x 238 cm). Private collection. Courtesy of the Fundación Juan Soriano y Marek Keller A.C., Mexico City

muse of inspiration behind him. Observing him, and the children, are two of the most significant figures in Soriano's life at this period, his sister Martha and Diego de Mesa.[76]

Within the realm of Soriano's erotic allegories of the 1940s, perhaps the most ambitious is the 1949 *Saint Jerome Mourned by Angels* (fig. 30). Tones of gold and blue predominate in this large canvas. The saint himself, a muscular nude, hovers on a cloud in the upper portion of the composition. A host of nude male and female angels surround him and his lion companion at the right. This work is a variation on the theme of the Temptation of Saint Jerome. In traditional images of this subject the saint often appears as an old man beset by alluring young women urging him to sin. Here, however, Jerome is threatened with arrows by two highly eroticized male angels (most of the female angels surround and caress the lion). More an orgy than a religious drama, this version of an episode of Saint Jerome's life serves as a vehicle for displaying the artist's expertise in anatomical rendering and heightened sexual suggestiveness.

All of the works discussed above incorporate dream-like or otherwise surprising elements. While they manifest a distinct taste for the unusual, none, with the possible exception of the 1944 lithograph, could be directly connected with the types of Surrealist expression brought to Mexico by the émigré artists. Each of these paintings evidences, nonetheless, Soriano's fluid approach to realistic representation, a characteristic he shared with a number of his Mexican contemporaries.

Soriano and Philadelphia

Soriano often described the importance of the many trips he made with friends to rural parts of Mexico during the late 1930s and 1940s.[77] There are various photographs that record these journeys (see fig. 7). A particularly interesting one shows the artist himself posing impishly as a baroque sculpture in a niche of the colonial parish church in Salamanca, Guanajuato (fig. 31).[78] This elaborate "installation" obviously required the participation of the artist's friends to place the ladder he used to ascend to this lofty position. The theatricality of this stunt is attested to by the presence of a person taking a picture of the smiling artist. The photographer is Henry Clifford, Curator of Paintings at the Philadelphia Museum of Art.[79]

Soriano remembered another trip, to Oaxaca, as

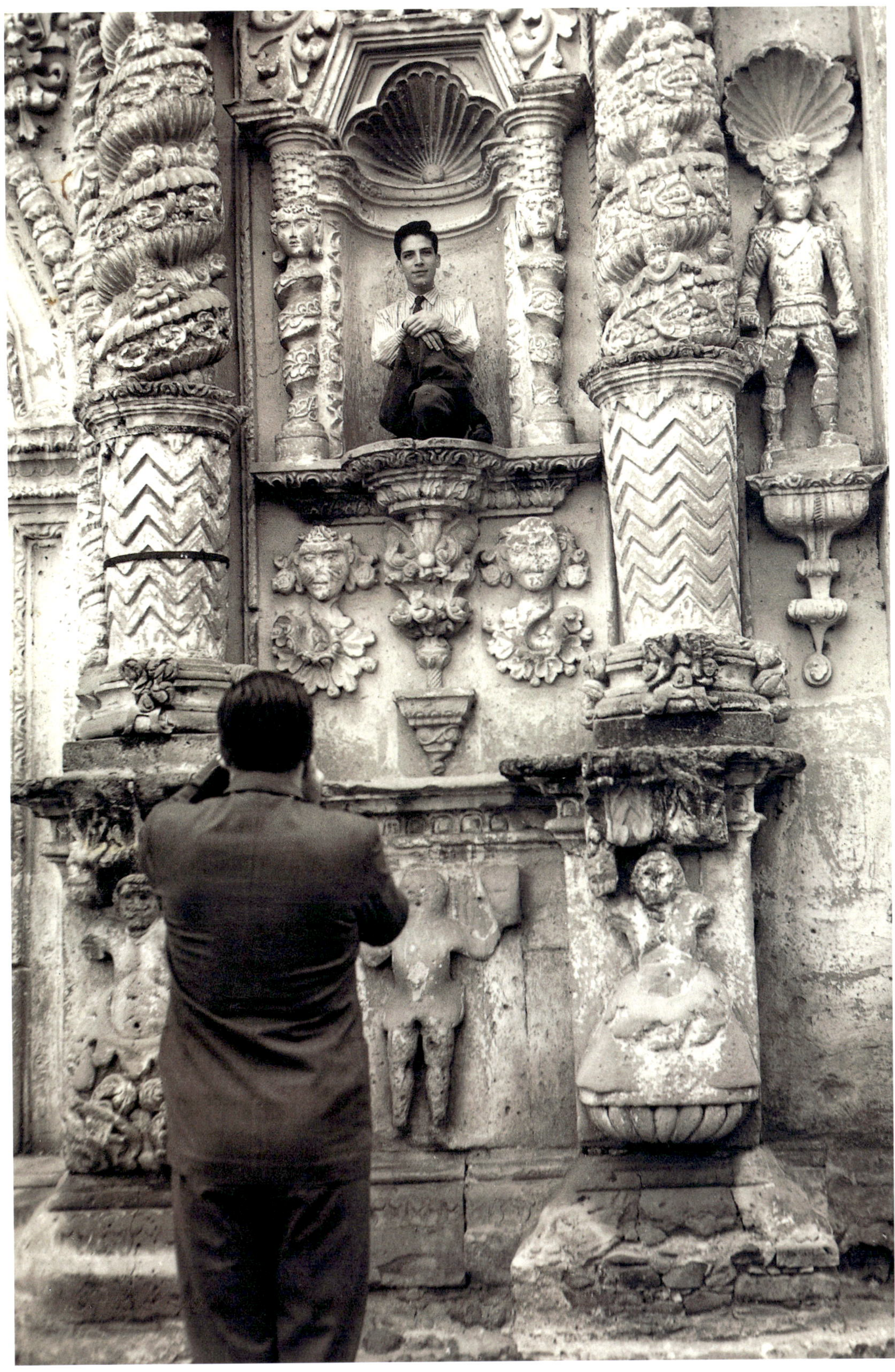

FIG. 31. Photographer unknown. Juan Soriano being photographed by Henry Clifford at the parish church, Salamanca, Guanajuato, 1943. Courtesy of the Fundación Juan Soriano y Marek Keller A.C., Mexico City

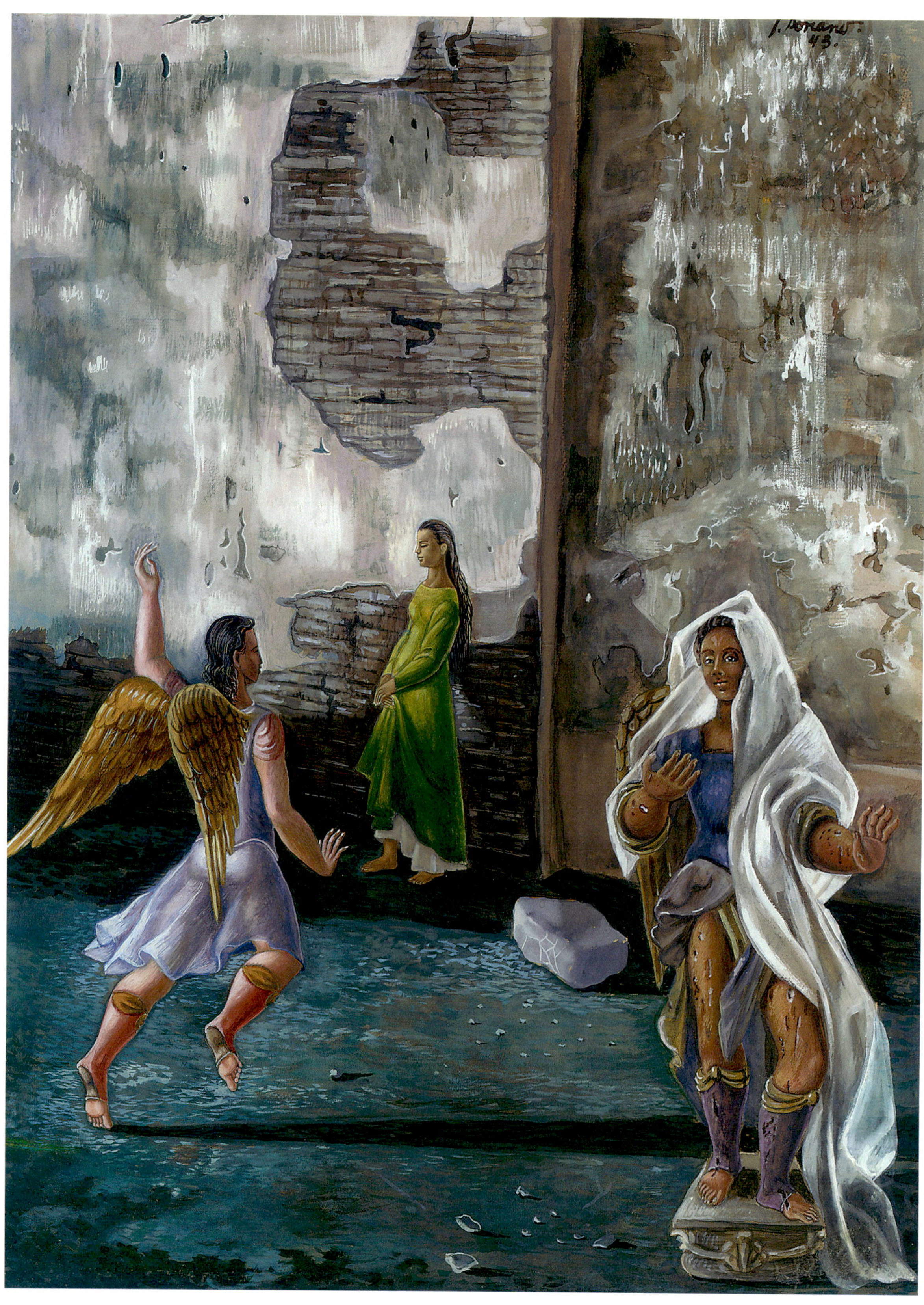

FIG. 32. *Recreation of Archangels*, 1943. Tempera on paper, 25$\frac{5}{8}$ x 20$\frac{1}{16}$ inches (65 x 51 cm). Collection of The Vergel Foundation, New York. Courtesy of the Fundación Juan Soriano y Marek Keller A.C., Mexico City

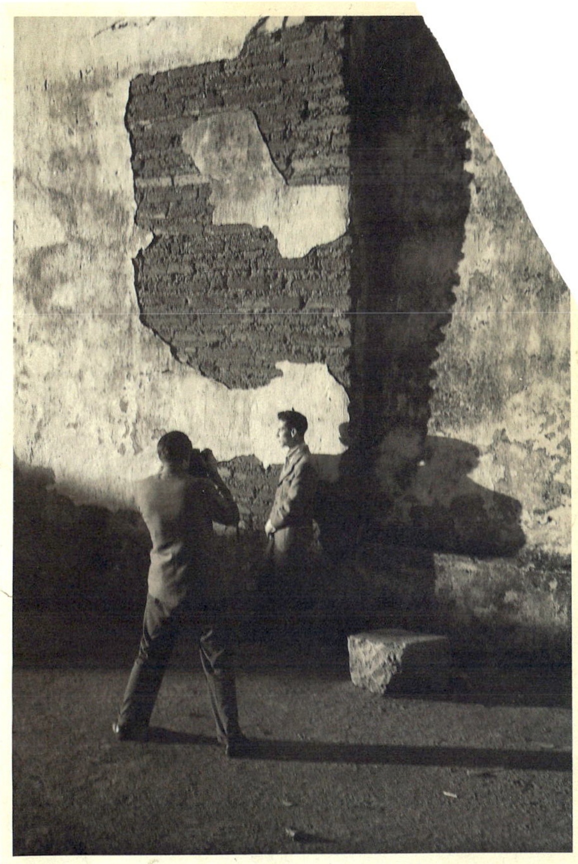

FIG. 33. Photographer unknown. Juan Soriano being photographed by Henry Clifford, 1943. Courtesy of the Fundación Juan Soriano y Marek Keller A.C., Mexico City

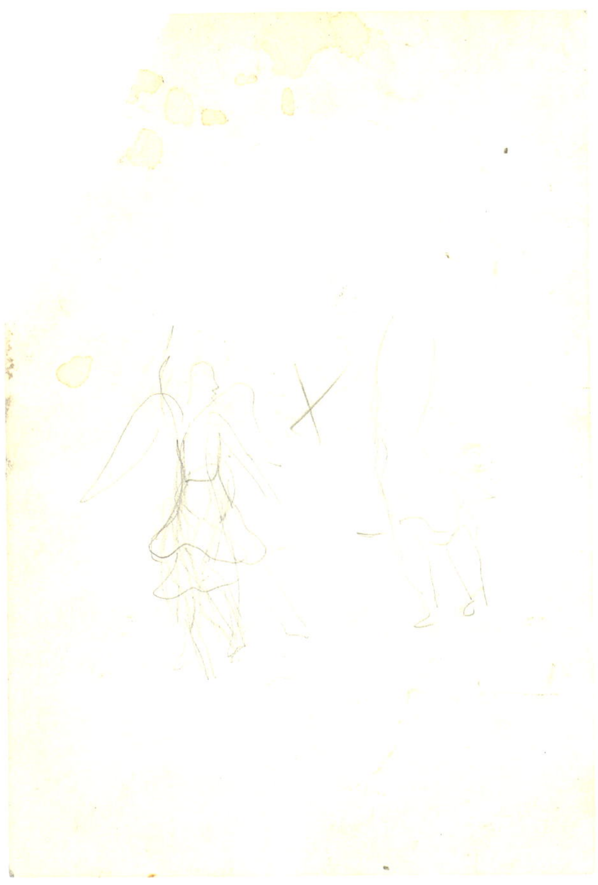

FIG. 34. Pencil drawing for *Recreation of Archangels*, 1943 (verso of fig. 33)

having been instrumental for the composition of one of his most arresting works of the period, *Recreation of Archangels* of 1943 (fig. 32). A photograph of Soriano posed against the wall "of a ruined monastery," as he described it (fig. 33), served as the inspiration for the figures in this tempera on paper of 1943 that includes two images of his beloved angels.[80] Of the three figures in the painting, however, only one is a "conventional" angel; another is a wooden statue, and the third, a woman posed against a wall, is the transformed figure of Soriano from the photograph, which again shows Clifford taking the picture. On the reverse is Soriano's initial sketch for the tempera (fig. 34).

Henry Clifford played a significant role as friend, collector, and promoter of Soriano's work throughout the 1940s. He was one of the most energetic advocates of modern Mexican art in the United States during the late 1930s and into the war years, a time when interest in this field was at an all-time high.[81] Americans had been fascinated by Mexican art since the 1920s, and, starting in the early 1930s, many important exhibitions of modern, colonial, ancient, and folk art from Mexico were organized in museums around the United States. One reason for the surge in interest was that the outbreak of the war prevented American art collectors from tapping into the European market; as a result, many turned their attentions to Latin America, especially to Mexico.[82] Building on an existing strength in Mexican colonial art at the Philadelphia Museum of Art, Clifford set out to create an equally distinguished modern Mexican collection.[83] In a letter to Inés Amor dated June 6, 1945, he stated, "Bit by bit I am building up a Mexican group and having two special galleries built and painted to receive

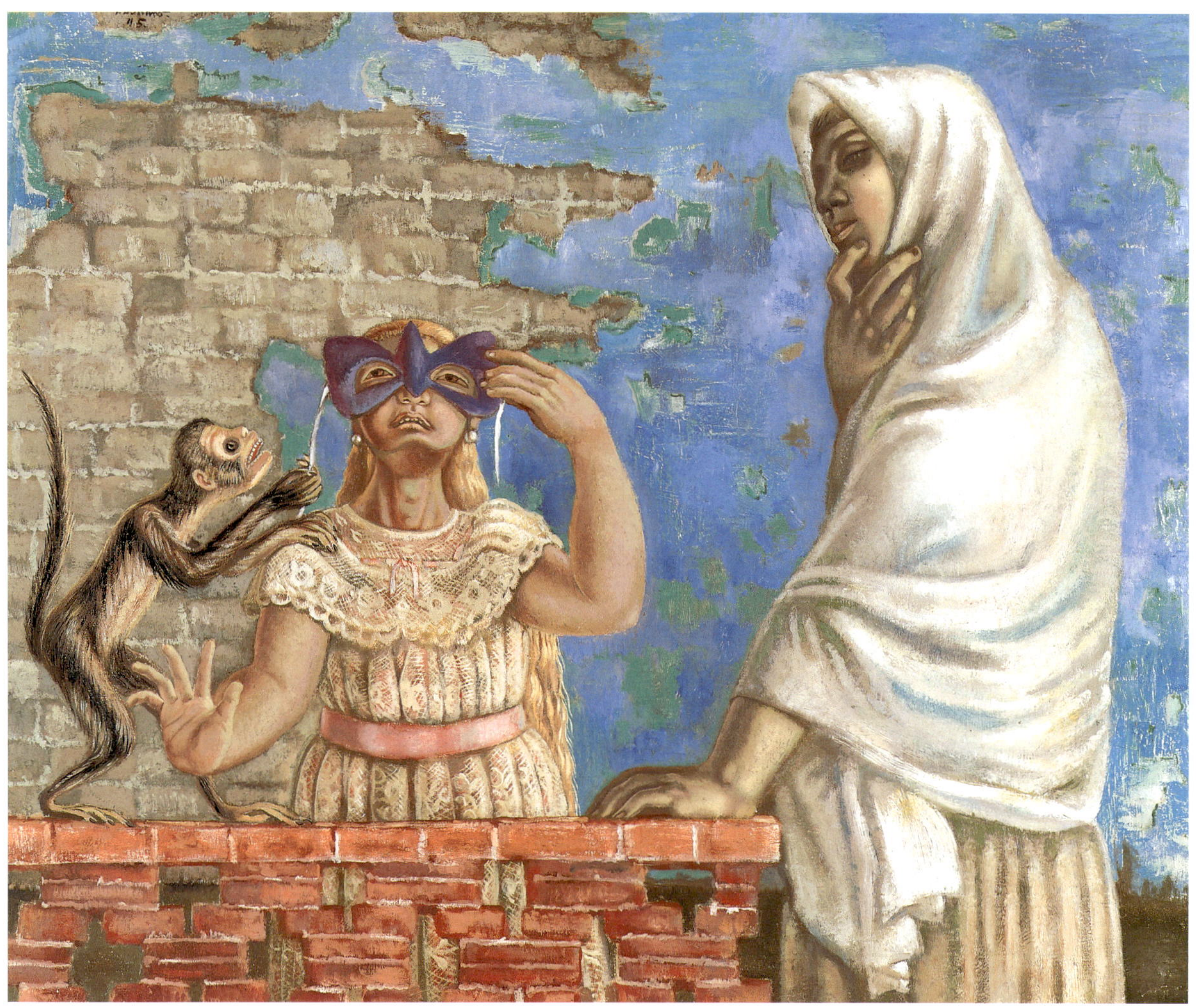

*FIG. 35. *Girl with a Mask*, 1945. Oil on canvas, 31⅝ x 39½ inches (80.3 x 100.3 cm). Philadelphia Museum of Art. Gift of Mrs. Herbert Cameron Morris, 1947-24-1

them."[84] Ultimately he succeeded in creating a strong corpus of modern Mexican paintings that includes excellent examples by most of the well-known artists of that period.

Clifford spent as much time as possible in Mexico. Although he rented an apartment in Mexico City for his visits to the capital, his real home was the large colonial-era house in the town of Jonacatepec, Morelos, which he had lovingly restored and filled with "a fabulous collection of wonderful Mexican antique furniture and art."[85]

The three-decade-long correspondence between Clifford and Inés Amor (now in the archives of the Philadelphia Museum of Art and Galería de Arte Mexicano) contains many references to the importance of Juan Soriano to both correspondents. In a letter of January 13, 1944, for example, Amor writes of her concern for the artist's delicate health and financial situation (she had recently opened a bank account for him).[86] On April 20, 1945, she told Clifford about the artist's solo show at her gallery: "Juan's exhibition was incredible. It brought hundreds of visitors, had extraordinary write-ups and 21 sales out of the 25 paintings shown. He is very happy about it all and also about his health, which has improved a lot."[87]

Much of the correspondence from the year 1943 concerns the large exhibition that Clifford had organized (with the collaboration of Amor) for the Philadelphia Museum of Art.[88] *Mexican Art Today* traveled extensively throughout the United States and

Canada after leaving Philadelphia, and was one of the most ambitious shows devoted exclusively to modern Mexican painting, prints, and photography up to that time.[89] The catalogue included a lengthy essay by Luis Cardoza y Aragón entitled "Hurricane or Flame," translated into English by Clifford's wife, Esther Rowland Clifford. Two works by Soriano were in the show, the 1938 *Dead Girl* (see fig. 36) and the 1942 *Burial* (see fig. 41). He, along with Cantú, Ricardo Martínez, Meza, and Francisco Gutiérrez, is listed in the catalogue as part of the "Third Generation," a subcategory representing the "International Approach."

Two years later the Knoedler Gallery in New York presented the exhibition *Mexican Painting* from November 6 to 24, organized with the assistance of Amor, who attended the opening with Soriano, Clifford having written to her on October 12: "Why don't you bring Juan as your secretary or body-guard (!) or some such? He would be happier here with you than with anyone."[90] At this time, Soriano was able to view contemporary American art in the New York galleries and museums, and most likely was able to meet some of the people, such as Alfred H. Barr, Jr., Director of the Museum of Modern Art, and Lincoln Kirstein, who had recently exhibited and purchased his work. Kirstein held the title of Consultant on Latin American Art at the Modern at the time and had included Soriano's gouache *Child with Bird* (see fig. 19) in his 1943 exhibition *The Latin American Collection of the Museum of Modern Art*.[91]

After the 1943 *Mexican Art Today* show, Clifford, who with his wife would donate some key Mexican works to the Philadelphia Museum of Art, including the *Dead Girl*, continued (with the help of Amor) to place pictures by Soriano in important American collections.[92] Of the poetically enigmatic painting *Girl with a Mask* (fig. 35), now in Philadelphia, he wrote, amusingly, to Amor on December 12, 1945: "I got a friend of mine, Mrs. Herbert [Cameron] Morris to go to New York and see your show [at Knoedler]. I told her of Juan's *Two Figures & Monkey*—or whatever the official title is—& she fell in love with it & bought it. . . . Her husband makes a brand called TASTEYCAKE [*sic*] so she naturally has $$$$$!"[93]

Clifford's many letters to Amor continued arriving in Mexico City until the fall of 1974, when he died on November 14 in Lausanne at age seventy. They attest to the author's sustained concern with Juan Soriano and describe his interest in the vitality of Mexican art. They include tantalizing gossip about mutual friends on two continents and express Clifford's deep affection for Amor. Her letters to him are equally filled with art-world information, details of minor scandals, and personal warmth.[94]

Niñas Muertas

"While still an adolescent, he took his brushes and surprised Mexican painters with his now-famous *Dead Girl* [fig. 36]. A terrible grace animates her twitching lips, the tender and anguished toes, the simple flowers and the solitary hands that pray after death."[95] These words of critic José Luis Martínez describe the most famous work in Soriano's first one-artist exhibition in August 1941 and his best-known picture in the Philadelphia Museum of Art. It is also his most often reproduced and discussed early work. Its genesis was a specific event witnessed by Soriano and Lola Alvarez Bravo on a 1938 trip to Veracruz: "We were walking down a street and were both struck by a singular scene, a dead child dressed like an angel, laid out in a front window of a house for everyone to see. She had just died, and the family wanted their neighbors to know. I was riveted by this and soon began doing a painting of this girl."[96] His painting does not romanticize or beautify death. It even has a subtly grotesque element in the bit of cotton inserted into the child's nose to prevent postmortem excretions. Her dress is a dull brown, contrasting with the bright color of the roses, magnolias, and marigolds (traditionally used since Aztec times in funerary rituals) surrounding the body. The disembodied hands above, praying for the soul of the child, add an additional air of the unreal.

The starkness of the scene as well as the wiry quality of the drawing had an impact on critics and reviewers. The technique of the *Dead Girl* also influenced Soriano's fellow painter Ricardo Martínez. Martínez, another artist who showed at the Galería de Arte Mexicano, was described by Amor as having been under the protective wing of Soriano in the first years of the 1940s. Although two years older, he was "supported by Soriano, from whom he learned many

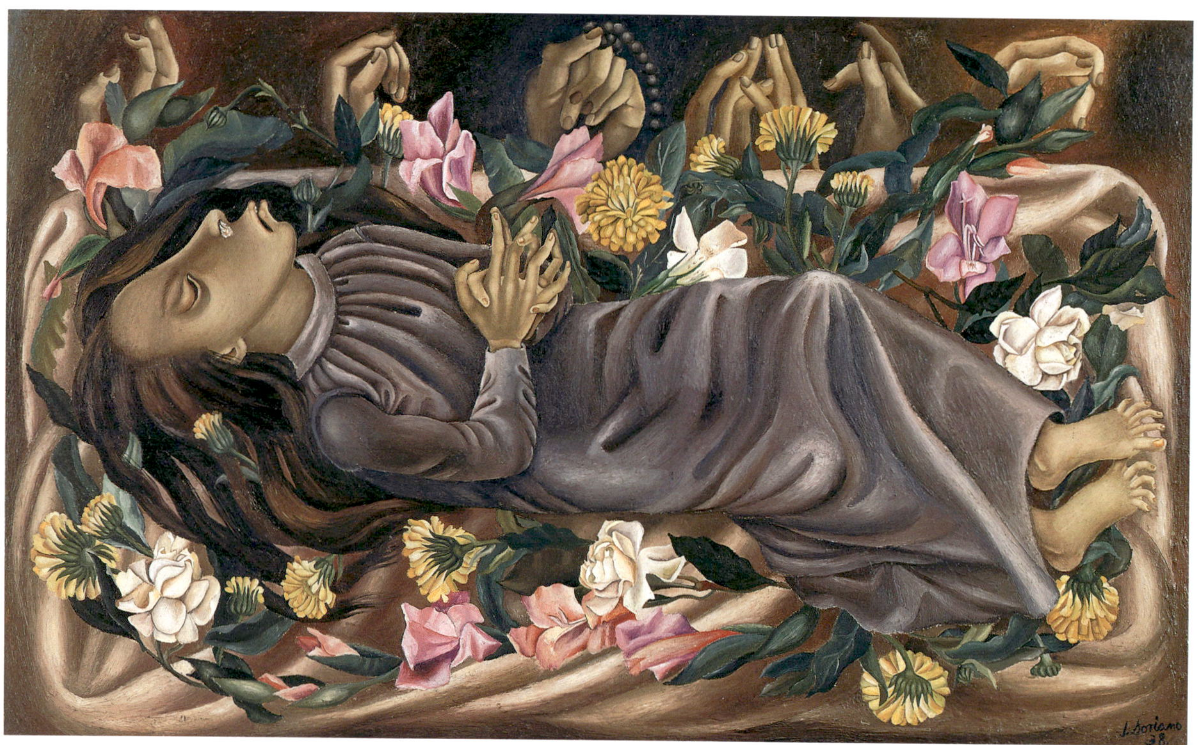

*FIG. 36. *The Dead Girl*, 1938. Oil on panel, 18½ x 31½ inches (47 x 80 cm). Philadelphia Museum of Art. Gift of Mr. and Mrs. Henry Clifford, 1947-29-3

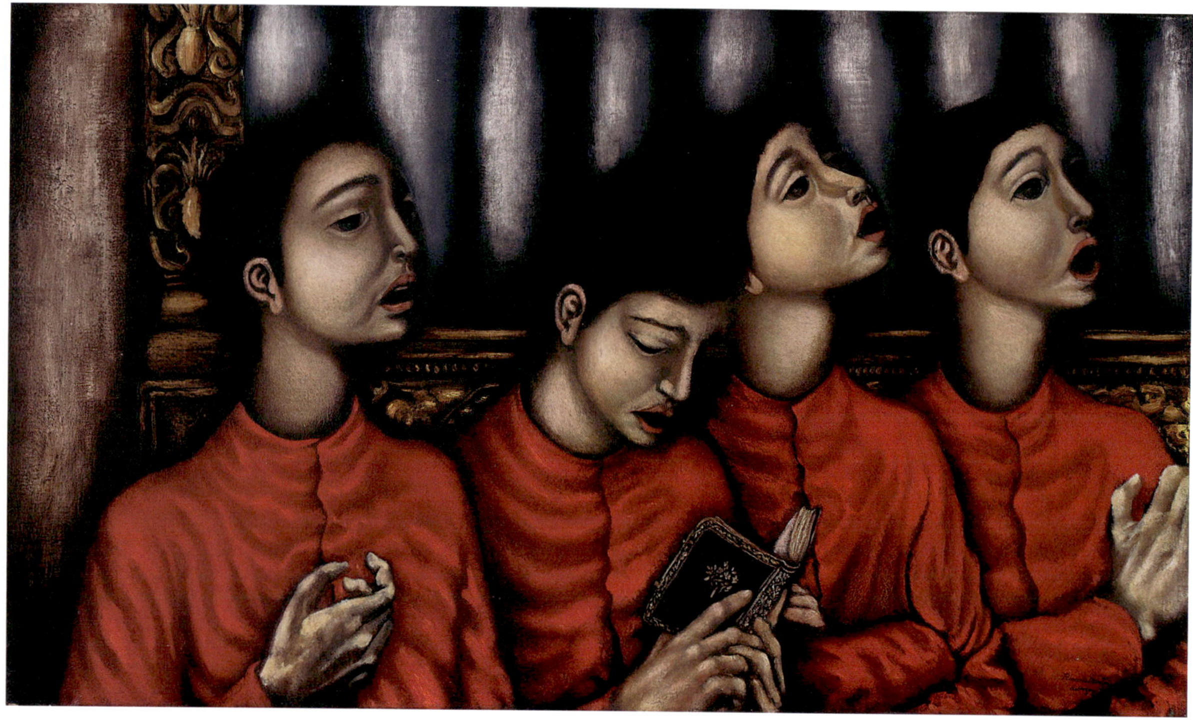

FIG. 37. Ricardo Martínez de Hoyos (Mexican, born 1918). *Choir Boys*, 1942. Oil on canvas, 20½ x 34⅝ inches (52.1 x 87.9 cm). Philadelphia Museum of Art. Gift of Mr. and Mrs. Henry Clifford, 1947-29-2

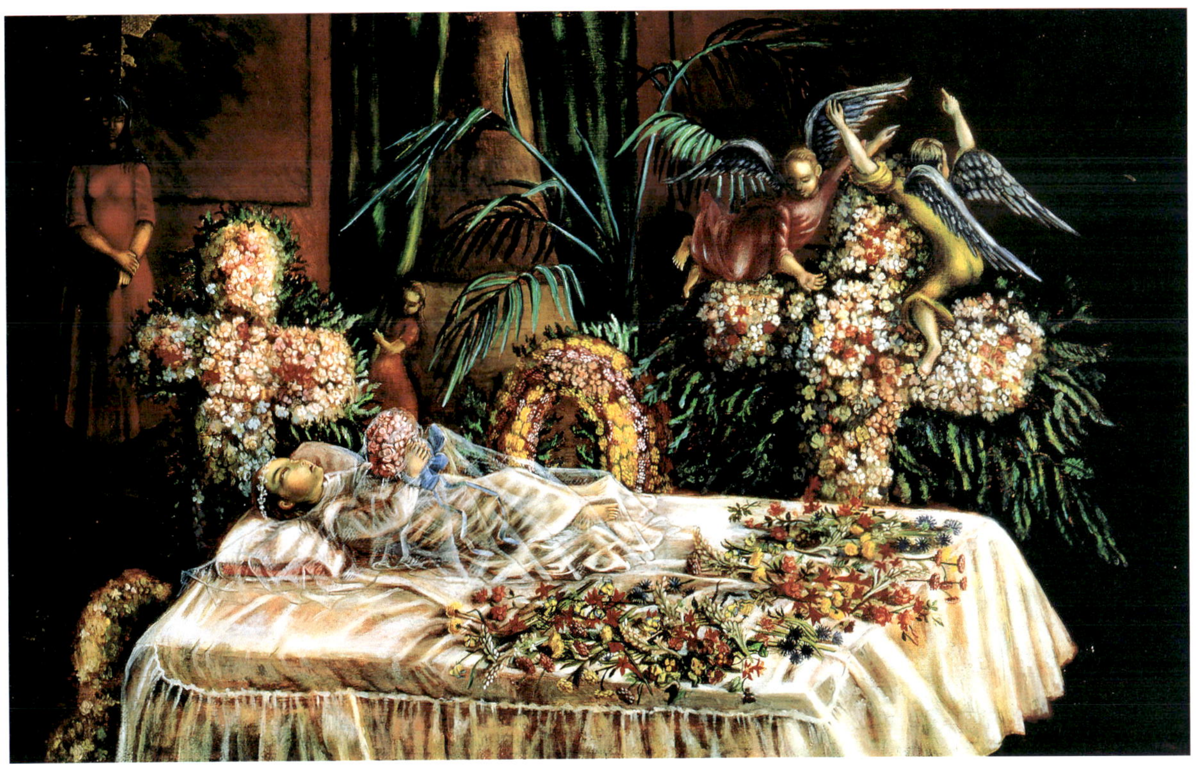

*FIG. 38. *The Dead Girl*, 1944. Oil on wood, 22 x 36 inches (55.9 x 91.4 cm). Gilcrease Museum, Tulsa, Oklahoma

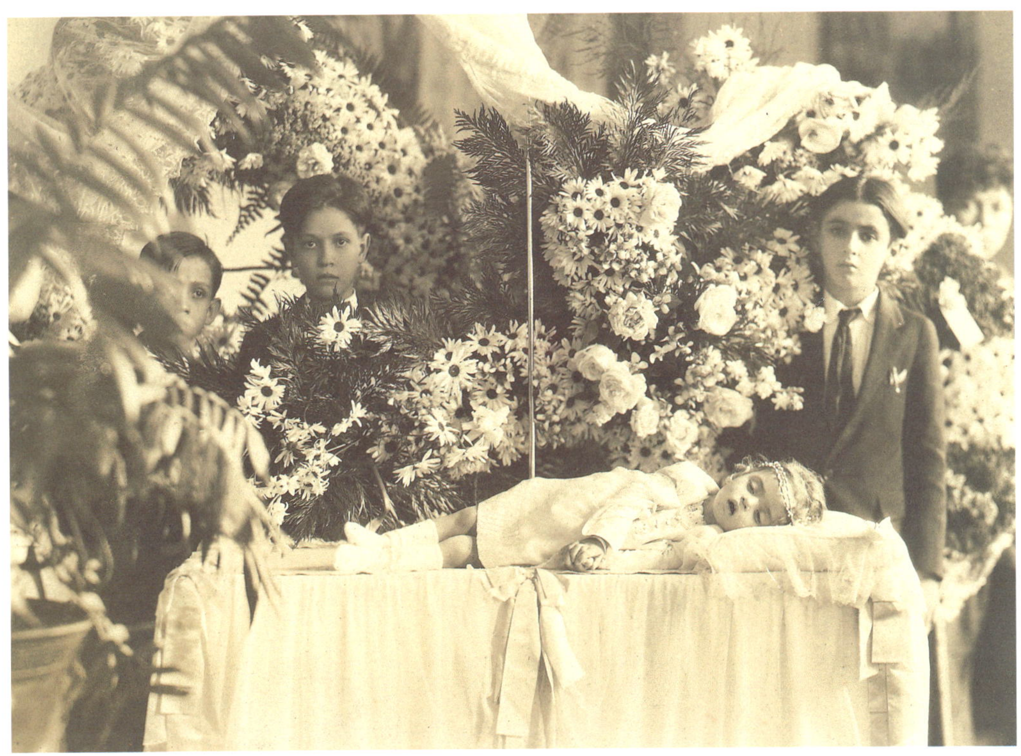

FIG. 39. *The Dead Child*. Mexican, c. 1890–1900. Albumen print, 4½ x 6½ inches (11.4 x 16.5 cm). Private collection

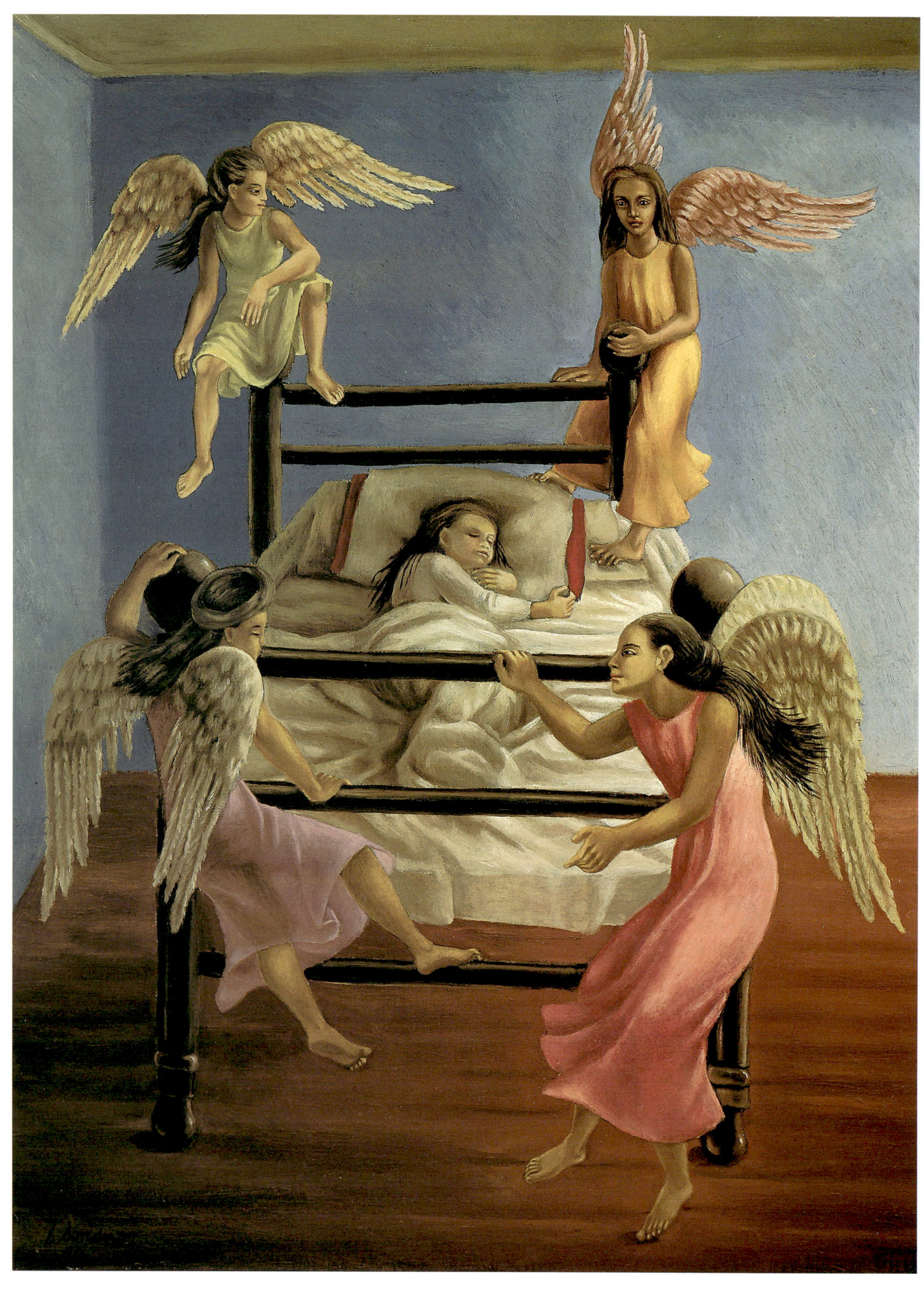

*FIG. 40. *My Bed Has Four Little Corners*, 1941. Oil on canvas, 25⅝ x 20¹⁄₁₆ inches (65 x 51 cm). Museo Andrés Blaisten, Mexico City

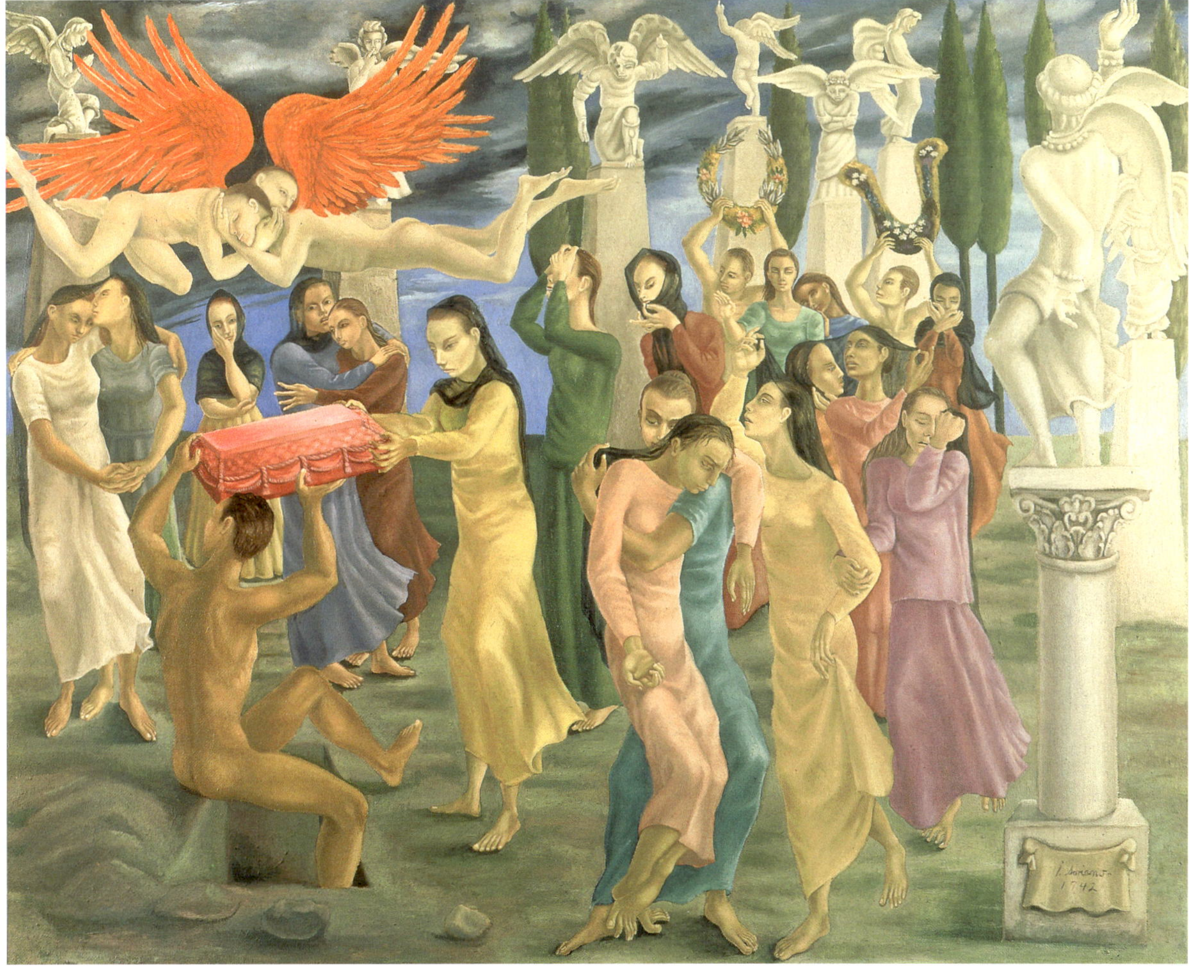

FIG. 41. *The Burial*, 1942. Oil on Masonite, 36⅝ x 47¼ inches (93 x 120 cm). Private collection. Courtesy of the Fundación Juan Soriano y Marek Keller A.C., Mexico City

things."[97] While Martínez later distinguished himself as a painter of large, rounded, semiabstract forms, his early works, such as another Clifford gift to the Museum—the 1942 *Choir Boys* (fig. 37)—testify to a deeply shared sensibility with his younger friend. His choir boys exude a sense of contemplation and melancholy similar to that of Soriano's dead girl.

The *Dead Girl* forms part of a long-standing visual tradition in Latin America that had particular strength in Mexico in both painting and photography.[98] Several of Soriano's contemporaries made well-known depictions of dead babies, including Siqueiros (*Portrait of a Living and a Dead Girl*, 1931; Museo Soumaya, Mexico City), Kahlo (*The Deceased Dimas*, 1937; Fundación Dolores Olmedo Patiño), and Julio Castellanos, whose *Angel Kidnappers* of 1943 was sold to the Museum of Modern Art through the influence of Henry Clifford.

Soriano's *Dead Girl* of 1944 (fig. 38) is one of his most elaborate compositions of this series. Its profusion of flowers serves as a sharp contrast to its sense of silence and loss. Angels carry two immense crosses of roses, wreaths decorate the sides of the bed, and the deceased child holds a bouquet. The bed itself is covered in petals. This work emphasizes the popular belief that in death a child assumes the guise of an *angelito* and is thus dressed for its wake in white. The painting, sold by Amor to the American collector Thomas Gilcrease and now in the Tulsa, Oklahoma, museum that bears his name, comes closest in spirit to the many infant postmortem photographs that became common in the later nineteenth century. The comparison to an anonymous albumen print of about

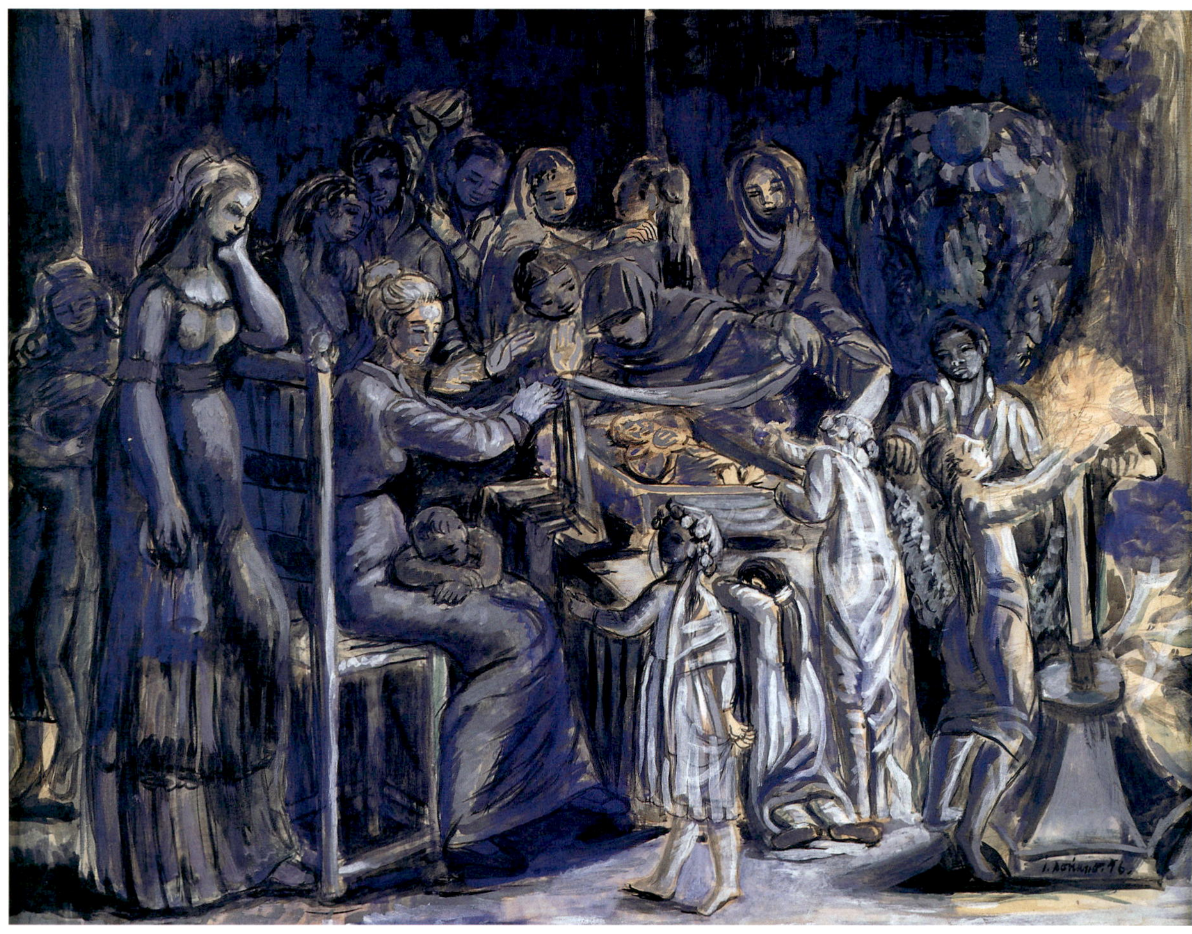

FIG. 42. *The Dead Girl (The Wake)*, 1946. Tempera on paper, 18⅛ x 28 inches (46 x 71 cm). Private collection. Courtesy of the Fundación Juan Soriano y Marek Keller A.C., Mexico City

1890–1900 (fig. 39) is instructive. Both images share an aura of deep melancholy, and both display a profusion of flowers, whose sweet scent would accompany the spirit of the dead into the next life. Soriano's painting and the photograph also both contain images of family members as mute witnesses to the painful loss of the child.

While Soriano's 1941 *My Bed Has Four Little Corners* (fig. 40) does not directly address the theme of infant mortality (still a problem in Mexico at this time), it is nonetheless related to his series of *niños muertos.* Here we see a sleeping child surrounded by angels on all four sides of her diminutive bed. The strong color contrasts of blues, pinks, and whites call attention to the intensity and tenderness of the image. The title derives from a folk refrain popular in Guadalajara. It has several variants, but the most well known is:

Four little corners
Has my bed
Four little angels
Guard it for me
I go to sleep with God
And wake up with Him
With the Virgin Mary
And with the Holy Spirit.[99]

Other examples from the painter's series of *niños muertos* are more elaborate in their allegorical suggestions. *The Burial* of 1942 (fig. 41), for example, displays none of the quotidian sobriety of the above-mentioned images. It presents, instead, the event as part of a vast pageant or theatrical performance, complete with clothed and nude participants, cenotaphs supporting marble angels, and a pair of lifelike mourning angels embracing in a gesture of mutual grieving in the sky. No less elaborate but more reflective of the real world is *The Dead Girl* (also called *The Wake*) of 1946, now in the collection of the Museo de Arte Moderno, Mexico City, the sketch for which is illustrated here (fig. 42). Many family members, both male and female, press in on the deceased baby who lies in a small coffin draped by a gauzy sheet. The cloth is lifted by mourning women, one of whom is Lola Alvarez Bravo (seated at the left of the child), making this image the only one in the series to depict a friend of the artist. Alvarez Bravo is not known to have had a child who died in infancy, so this painting takes on an even more mysterious quality than usual.

While Soriano did not paint series of deceased children after the 1940s, the subject of death and the depiction of skulls and skeletons nonetheless continued to be a compelling one for him. This theme stayed with him during his years of residence abroad, beginning in 1951, first in Rome and later in Paris. Death imagery nourished and entertained him, and he later portrayed death as an amusement, a challenge as well as an inevitability.[100]

Conclusion

The art dealer and friend of Soriano, Malú Block, with whom he exhibited beginning in the 1960s at the Galería Juan Martín in Mexico City, stated that one of the most significant things about Soriano's art in the 1940s was that it "served as a bridge between the Mexican School and the so-called *Ruptura*."[101] She indicated that the openness of his attitude and his liberal imagination served as a lesson for other artists, opening doors and setting an example for experimentation. Block's use of the term *ruptura* refers to the movements of the 1950s and 1960s that, while without a cohesive pictorial style, were characterized principally by a desire to create a rupture with the past and to respond to increasingly strong contacts with artists abroad. Indeed, Soriano's career itself took many radical turns starting in the early 1950s, embracing (at least briefly) total gestural abstraction and, ultimately, a form of lyrical realism that characterized his painting, drawing, prints, and sculpture until his death in 2006.

Soriano's art of the late 1930s and 1940s represents a key period in his aesthetic formation, which critics have tended to look at through the lens of a strictly Mexican framework, using it as a benchmark in a continual process of the de-folklorization of Mexican painting. While this is arguably true, we should also ask questions about the further affinities and visual affiliations with other traditions that Soriano may have had at the time, including the parallels with the art of Balthus that have been discussed. Other European realists may be examined for corresponding kinships. For example, the art of the more conservative former members of the School of Montparnasse, such as the portraits, still lifes, and cityscapes of the Polish-born French painter Moise Kisling (1891–1953), is called to mind. Yet it may be equally tempting to suggest Soriano's connections with the work of some of the North American realists who were active and well known in the 1940s. We may look, for instance, to some of the painters associated with American Scene painting, magic realism, or even American Surrealism as having shared affinities with their Mexican counterpart. These may include Paul Cadmus, Philip Evergood, Jared French, and George Tooker, whose paintings Soriano may well have observed in New York galleries during his visits or in the art periodicals he saw in Mexico.[102] It is less important, however, to make specific connections between individual foreign artists and the production of Soriano at this time than it is to look at his visual output in the wider context of a well-established, transnational taste for oneiric realism.[103] Soriano's contribution in the years up to 1950 thus truly forms what Malú Block defined as a "bridge," yet one that may be more accurately said to span considerably wider chasms than those within the Mexican art world. Most significantly, it forms a contribution to a larger aesthetic dialogue that developed both north and south and across many cultural divides.

Notes

All translations are by the author, except where noted.

1 This drawing was a fiftieth-birthday gift for the art patron and collector Marte R. Gómez, Mexican Minister of Agriculture and Development. Many other prominent Mexican artists of the day also celebrated Gómez's birthday with self-portrait drawings. The majority of these are in the Museo Soumaya, Mexico City.

2 Among the important recent Latin American exhibitions are *The Arts in Latin America, 1492–1820*, and *Mexico and Modern Printmaking: A Revolution in the Graphic Arts, 1920 to 1950*, both in 2006. As early as 1908, the Museum organized the exhibition *Mexican Antiquities*.

3 Historians and critics of modern Mexican art, such as Esther Acevedo, Mary K. Coffey, Karen Cordero Reiman, Olivier Debroise, Anna Indych-López, James Oles, and Adriana Zavala, are concerned with issues of patronage, the art market, colonialism and post-colonialism, and gender in discussing the work of many of Soriano's contemporaries. See, for example, the four-volume anthology *Hacia otra historia del arte en México* (Mexico City: Consejo Nacional para la Cultura y las Artes, 2001–4).

4 Elena Poniatowska, *Juan Soriano, niño de mil años* (Mexico City: Plaza y Janés, 1998), p. 60.

5 Jaime Moreno Villarreal, in *Celebración a Juan Soriano* (Puebla: Fundación Amparo, 2005), pp. 82–83, offers an extensive description of Chucho Reyes's "team" of young forgers of "colonial" religious paintings and portraits, saying that when the pictures were ready for sale the group would take them into the patio of Reyes's house and urinate on them to make them "appear older."

6 Ibid., p. 82.

7 Diana Briuolo Destéfano, in *Juan Soriano: Pintor de antiguos y nuevos dilemas* (Mexico City: Consejo Nacional para la Cultura y las Artes, 1997), p. 12, stated that Reyes purchased the image of a *niña muerta*. The whereabouts of this work is unknown.

8 Olivier Debroise, "Jesús Guerrero Galván (notas para un estudio comparativo)," in Museo de Arte Moderno, Mexico City, *Jesús Guerrero Galván (1910–1973): De personas y personajes*, exh. cat. (Mexico City: Museo de Arte Moderno, 1994), p. 14.

9 Ibid., p. 23. Debroise notes that in the 1940s Chucho Reyes, "a pillar of the Guadalajara bohemia," lived next door to the Galería de Arte Mexicano on the calle Milán in Mexico City, which was another reason that the artists from Jalisco congregated there.

10 Carlos Monsiváis, "Mínima crónica: Juan Soriano en sus 70 años," in Octavio Paz et al., *Juan Soriano: Retratos y esculturas* (Mexico City: Grupo Azabache, 1991), p. 53. This view of painting in Jalisco at the time applies to only a certain portion of artists working first in Guadalajara and then in the capital. There is the other side of this picture, represented, most outstandingly, by the towering figure of the Jalisco native José Clemente Orozco.

11 Juan Soriano, interview with the author, Mexico City, March 18–19, 2004.

12 Poniatowska, *Soriano*, p. 43.

13 Soriano, interview with the author.

14 Sergio Pitol, *Juan Soriano: El perpetuo rebelde* (Mexico City: Consejo Nacional para la Cultura y las Artes, 1993), p. 8.

15 Adolfo Best Maugard, *Método de dibujo: Tradición, resurgimiento, y evolución del arte mexicano* (Mexico City: Secretaría de Educación Pública, 1923).

16 Alvarez Bravo included the head of Soriano in one of her experimental Surrealist photomontages, *The Dream of the Drowned*, of about 1945. See Elizabeth Ferrer, *Lola Alvarez Bravo* (New York: Aperture, 2006), p. 131.

17 Teri Geis, "María Izquierdo: Retrato de Juan Soriano, 1939," in *Colección Andrés Blaisten: Arte moderno de México*, ed. James Oles and Fausto Ramírez (Mexico City: Universidad Nacional Autónoma de México, 2005), p. 186.

18 Poniatowska, *Soriano*, p. 142.

19 Octavio G. Barreda, "Juan Soriano," *El hijo pródigo*, no. 25 (April 15, 1945); reprinted in Pitol, *Soriano*, pp. 157–58.

20 Ibid., p. 157.

21 The term "Mexican School" is an imprecise and, essentially, confusing one that has been employed in a variety of ways to describe many aspects of Mexican art of the 1920s to the 1950s. Some critics define it as referring to painting and graphic work from the period following the end of the armed conflicts that constituted the Mexican Revolution. Others use the term to separate the painters whose principal contributions were on canvas from the muralists. I prefer not to use this term when at all possible, while acknowledging that, if the school had existed as an entity, its principal characteristics would include representations of what ultimately became clichéd images of Mexican "types" (mainly rural, but at times urban) or "picturesque" objects that could be understood as synecdoches of *mexicanidad*. On the formation of the

stereotypes of the "Escuela Mexicana," see Karen Cordero Reiman, "Constructing a Modern Mexican Art, 1910–1940," in *South of the Border: Mexico in the American Imagination, 1914–1947*, by James Oles (Washington, DC: Smithsonian Institution Press, 1993), pp. 10–47.

22 Translation by Eliot Weinberger.

23 Paz remained in Mexico City until 1945, when he left for over twenty-three years in the diplomatic service.

24 "I loved reading and would read all the time. Even when I was about eight years old, my teachers would go off and leave me to teach the class, so I had to read a lot." Soriano, interview with the author.

25 Poniatowska, *Soriano*, p. 88.

26 Octavio Paz, "Price and Meaning," in *Essays on Mexican Art*, by Octavio Paz (New York: Harcourt Brace, 1993), p. 290.

27 "I never learned much in drawing class, but I loved the theater and went as much as possible to the Teatro Principal when the designers were painting the stage sets. They asked me to help them and I did." Soriano, interview with the author.

28 Soriano's most outstanding contribution to Mexican theater was his participation in the company known as Poesía en Voz Alta during the 1950s, an episode that falls outside the scope of this essay. See Roni Unger, *Poesía en Voz Alta* (Mexico City: Universidad Nacional Autónoma de México, 2006).

29 Alberto Dallal, *La danza contra la muerte* (Mexico City: Universidad Nacional Autónoma de México, 1979); see pt. 2, "La danza moderna en México," pp. 77–95.

30 Soriano did at least two portraits of Amalia Hernández in 1946 (oil on canvas and tempera on paper). Other dance- and theater-world subjects include, in 1948, Guillermina Bravo (founder of the Ballet Nacional de México) and the playwright and novelist Elena Garro (first wife of Octavio Paz and sister-in-law of Soriano's fellow painter Jesús Guerrero Galván), and, in 1975, the French choreographer Maurice Béjart. All of the above-mentioned works are in private collections with the exception of the portrait of Elena Garro, which is in Fundación Juan Soriano y Marek Keller A.C., Mexico City.

31 They published articles on avant-garde literature and art in their magazine *Los Contemporáneos* from June 1928 to January 1931. See the seven-volume facsimile edition *Los Contemporáneos* (Mexico City: Fondo de Cultura Económica, 1981).

32 Laura González Matute, "El arte de la posrevolución: Atmósfera renovada," in *Arte moderno de México, 1900–1950*, ed. Luis Martín Lozano, exh. cat. (Mexico City: Antiguo Colegio de San Ildefonso, 2000), pp. 55–74.

33 As an indicator of the animosity toward the homosexuality of some of the Contemporáneos, Diego Rivera is reported to have called them *maricas* (faggots) in a public lecture in 1928, as cited by the literary critic Ermilo Abreu Gómez in his essay "Contemporáneos," in the anthology *Las revistas literarias de México* (Mexico City: Instituto Nacional de Bellas Artes, Departamento de Literatura, 1963), p. 166. See also Adriana Zavala, "Tamayo's Women: Figures of an Alternative Modernism," in *Tamayo: A Modern Icon Reinterpreted*, ed. Diana C. Du Pont, exh. cat. (Santa Barbara: Santa Barbara Museum of Art, 2007), pp. 206, 222 n. 20.

34 See, for example, his forthright discussion of how his sexuality affected his early life in Poniatowska, *Soriano*, pp. 32–35, 49–50, 53–55.

35 See MacKinley Helm's introduction to *Modern Mexican Painters: A Loan Exhibition of Their Works Organized by the Institute of Modern Art, Boston*, exh. cat. (Boston: The Institute of Modern Art, 1941), pp. 10–15. This exhibition traveled to five other U.S. cities in 1942. Shortly thereafter Helm's well-known study of Mexican art with the same title as the exhibition was published by Harper.

36 Ibid., p. 55, no. 39.

37 For the most recent analysis of Alvarez Bravo's work (and for further bibliography), see Ferrer, *Lola Alvarez Bravo*.

38 Soriano, interview with the author.

39 Ibid.

40 Poniatowska, *Soriano*, p. 96.

41 Museo Nacional Centro de Arte Reina Sofía, Madrid, *Juan Soriano: Retrospectiva, 1937–1997*, exh. cat. (Madrid: Museo Nacional Centro de Arte Reina Sofía, 1997), p. 258.

42 Soriano, interview with the author.

43 Chano Urueta, "La transcendental exposición de la L.E.A.R.," *Hoy*, May 19, 1936. Clipping, Fundación Juan Soriano y Marek Keller Archives, Mexico City.

44 Soriano later criticized his colleague Santos Balmori for having retouched the painting discussed in Urueta's article, making it more folkloric and more *mexicanista* than he had intended. See Poniatowska, *Soriano*, pp. 70–71.

45 Pitol, *Soriano*, p. 12.

46 The artist says that Xavier Villaurrutia remarked that his portraits at this time were "sculpted, not painted." Ibid.

47 Like Soriano, González Serrano, from Jalisco, had studied with Francisco Rodríguez in Guadalajara before leaving for Mexico City in 1932. If he had not met Soriano in Guadalajara, he certainly encountered him later in the capital. Serrano's well-known still life in the Museo Andrés Blaisten—*Equilibrium (Projection, Margin)* of 1944—is particularly close to the background in Soriano's portrait of Rebeca Uribe and to some of his still lifes.

48 There are numerous European eye portraits in the collection of the Philadelphia Museum of Art. I am grateful to Dr. Susan Aberth for pointing out this tradition to me. Two eye portraits of the Mexican movie star María Félix

were sold at the auction of her estate at Christie's, New York, July 18, 2007, as lots 443 and 447.

49 Ramón Gaya, "Un siglo de retrato en México," *Letras de México*, no. 2 (February 15, 1943). Clipping, Fundación Juan Soriano y Marek Keller Archives, Mexico City.

50 This painting was a gift to the Philadelphia Museum of Art by Mrs. René d'Harnoncourt, wife of one of the great patrons and supporters of Mexican art and mother of the current director.

51 Soriano, interview with the author.

52 Pitol, *Soriano*, p. 14.

53 Lorenzo Varela, "Galería de Arte de la Librería de Cristal: Exposición Hispano-Mexicana," *Romance*, August 15, 1940. Clipping, Fundación Juan Soriano y Marek Keller Archives, Mexico City.

54 José Luis Martínez, "La pintura de Juan Soriano," *Letras de México*, 5th year, vol. 3, no. 8 (August 15, 1941). Clipping, Fundación Juan Soriano y Marek Keller Archives, Mexico City.

55 Ibid.

56 Nonetheless, Inés Amor, in her memoirs, stated that she had been selling work by Soriano since 1937, and she would continue to do so over the next three decades. Jorge Alberto Manrique and Teresa del Conde, *Una mujer en el arte mexicano: Memorias de Inés Amor*, rev. ed. (Mexico City: Universidad Nacional Autónoma de México, Instituto de Investigaciones Estéticas, 2005), p. 175.

57 Delmari Romero Keith, *Historia y testimonio: Galería de Arte Mexicano* (Mexico City: Ediciones Galería de Arte Mexicano, 1985), p. 293.

58 On the unique character of these provincial artists, see Edward J. Sullivan, "Naturalezas mexicanas," in *The Lure of the Object*, ed. Stephen Melville (Williamstown, MA: Sterling and Francine Clark Art Institute, 2005), pp. 59–71; and Sullivan, *The Language of Objects in the Art of the Americas* (New Haven: Yale University Press, 2007), pp. 102–10.

59 Soriano's links to Surrealism are discussed in the following section.

60 Teresa del Conde, "Juan Soriano en perspectiva," in *Juan Soriano y su obra*, by Carlos Fuentes and Teresa del Conde (Mexico City: Instituto Nacional de Bellas Artes, 1984), p. 13.

61 Soriano, interview with the author.

62 Among the many discussions of the exhibition and Surrealism's place in the Mexican art world of the 1940s, see Inés Amor's own account of the show in Manrique and del Conde, *Una mujer en el arte mexicano*, pp. 111–12; the essays in the exhibition catalogue Centro Atlántico de Arte Moderno, Madrid, *El surrealismo entre el viejo y nuevo mundo* (Madrid: Sala de Exposiciones de la Fundación Cultural Mapfre Vida, 1989); Martica Sawin, *Surrealism in Exile and the Beginning of the New York School* (Cambridge, MA: The MIT Press, 1997), ch. 7; as well as the controversial account in Ida Rodríguez Prampolini, *El surrealismo y el arte fantástico en México* (Mexico City: Universidad Nacional Autónoma de México, Instituto de Investigaciones Estéticas, 1983). See also the texts reproduced in Fabienne Bradu, *André Breton en México* (Mexico City: Editorial Vuelta, 1996), esp. pp. 232–45.

63 Poniatowska, *Soriano*, pp. 118–19.

64 As early as the late 1920s there is evidence of Surrealism's effect on Mexican painting. One notable instance is found in some of Tamayo's still lifes of 1928–29 in which odd juxtapositions of unrelated objects indicate his receptiveness to the movement as well as to Italian Metaphysical painting.

65 Rosamond Frost, "Mexicana of the Moment," *Art News*, no. 44 (November 15, 1945), p. 23. See also Sawin, *Surrealism in Exile*, pp. 286–87.

66 Works by Soriano have been included in several exhibitions examining Surrealism in Mexico, including Museo Nacional de Arte, Mexico City, *Los surrealistas en México*, exh. cat. (Mexico City: Museo Nacional de Arte, Instituto Nacional de Bellas Artes, 1986); and Museo Nacional de Arte, Mexico City, *Territorios de diálogo [entre los realismos y lo surreal]: España, México y Argentina, 1930–1945*, exh. cat. (Mexico City: Patronato del Museo Nacional de Arte, Instituto Nacional de Bellas Artes, 2006).

67 James Oles, "The Howl and the Flame: Tamayo's Wartime Allegories," in *Tamayo*, ed. Du Pont, p. 294.

68 Soriano, interview with the author.

69 Ibid.

70 Rodríguez Prampolini, *El surrealismo*, p. 90.

71 Included in this group portrait are Soriano's sisters Martha and Rosa, his mother, Amalia, and Dojean Lane (later Dojean Smithers, who, with her husband, the diplomat Sir Peter Smithers, collected his work), Lola Alvarez Bravo, Diego de Mesa, Elena Garro, Inés Amor, José Chávez Morado, John McAndrew, and the artist himself in the foreground.

72 Soriano, interview with the author.

73 On MacKinley Helm as collector and patron of Mexican art, see Catha Paquette, "U.S. Perceptions of Art Both Mexican and Modern: The Collecting, Publishing, and Curatorial Activities of MacKinley Helm," in *Patrocinio, colección, y circulación de las artes: XX Coloquio Internacional de Historia de Arte*, ed. Gustavo Curiel (Mexico City: Universidad Nacional Autónoma de México, Instituto de Investigaciones Estéticas, 1997), pp. 637–69.

74 In an unsigned article, "El nuevo romanticismo de Juan Soriano," *Hoy*, 1945 (n.d., n.p.), the author stated that Soriano "is akin in form to that other innocent demon Federico Cantú, but he is much more noble in his manner, more cherubic in his visions of color and his

contours." Clipping, Fundación Juan Soriano y Marek Keller Archives, Mexico City. Teresa del Conde also discusses this relationship in "Juan Soriano en perspectiva," p. 13.

75 Justino Fernández and Diego de Mesa, *Juan Soriano* (Mexico City: Universidad Nacional Autónoma de México, Dirección General de Publicaciones, 1976), p. 14.

76 The original owner of this painting was John McAndrew, friend of Soriano's, an architectural historian, Museum of Modern Art curator, and professor at Wellesley College. It was sold to him by Inés Amor. Mariana Pérez Amor, interview with the author, Mexico City, June 7, 2007.

77 Soriano, interview with the author.

78 This photograph has been previously published (Pitol, *Soriano*, p. 13), but the location is misidentified as Oaxaca. I am grateful to Clara Bargellini for clarifying that it represents the "right side (from our point of view) of the façade of the church of Salamanca, in the state of Guanajuato." Clara Bargellini, e-mail correspondence with the author, July 24, 2007.

79 Clifford served as Assistant Curator from 1932 to 1935, as Associate Curator from 1935 to 1942, and as Curator from 1942 until his retirement in 1964.

80 Soriano, interview with the author. See also Poniatowska, *Soriano*, p. 97.

81 Paquette, "U.S. Perceptions," stresses the importance of Helm in the formation of U.S. attitudes toward collecting Mexican art in the 1930s and 1940s. I would argue that while Clifford did not play as active a role as a writer on the subject, his curatorial and promotional activities were equally as significant within the U.S. market for many of the artists mentioned in this essay.

82 Oles, *South of the Border*; and Helen Delpar, *The Enormous Vogue of Things Mexican* (Tuscaloosa: University of Alabama Press, 1992).

83 On the formation of Philadelphia's colonial painting collection, see Clara Bargellini, "La Colección de la pintura colonial de Robert Lamborn en el Philadelphia Museum of Art," in *Patrocinio*, ed. Curiel, pp. 573–93.

84 Clifford to Amor, June 6, 1945. Galería de Arte Mexicano Archives, Mexico City.

85 Pérez Amor, interview with the author.

86 The original typed letter is in the Philadelphia Museum of Art Archives: Amor to Clifford, January 13, 1944. *Mexican Art Today* files. A copy of the letter is in the Galería de Arte Mexicano Archives, Mexico City.

87 Amor to Clifford, April 20, 1945. Galería de Arte Mexicano Archives, Mexico City.

88 Philadelphia Museum of Art, *Mexican Art Today*, exh. cat. (Philadelphia: Philadelphia Museum of Art, 1943).

89 Soriano's work was included in other large Mexican shows in the United States, including *Twenty Centuries of Mexican Art* at the Museum of Modern Art, New York (exh. cat. [New York: Museum of Modern Art, 1940]). Because of the lack of a printed checklist and no records in the exhibition's files at the museum, it cannot be determined which works by him were present.

90 Clifford to Amor, October 12, 1945. Galería de Arte Mexicano Archives, Mexico City.

91 This work was purchased for the Inter-American Fund from María Asúnsolo in 1942, perhaps by Barr on his 1942 Mexico trip; but it may also have been bought by Kirstein, who was himself in Mexico City in September 1942 at the end of a long Latin American journey to buy art for the Museum of Modern Art. The museum's archives do not state the name of the purchaser. I am grateful to Geaninne Guimarães at the Museum of Modern Art for her help with the provenance of this work and information on Soriano in the 1940 exhibition.

92 The photographic files of the Galería de Arte Mexicano contain numerous references to Soriano paintings and works on paper sold to North American collectors in all parts of the country in the 1940s. The location of many of these is currently unknown. It may be presumed that there are some significant works by Soriano in U.S. private collections that were sold by the Galería, many with help from Clifford.

93 Clifford to Amor, December 12, 1945. Galería de Arte Mexicano Archives, Mexico City. Clifford refers to the Knoedler exhibition as "your show." *Girl with a Mask*, also known as *Two Figures and a Monkey* and *Infinite Space*, was included in the exhibition. Mrs. Morris donated other important Mexican paintings to Philadelphia, including Tamayo's 1943 *Mad Dog*.

94 A small portion of this correspondence is reproduced in Romero Keith, *Historia y testimonios*, pp. 61–70.

95 Martínez, "La pintura de Juan Soriano," n.p.

96 Soriano, interview with the author.

97 Manrique and del Conde, *Una mujer en el arte mexicano*, p. 184.

98 See Sullivan, *The Language of Objects*, pp. 117–45.

99 I am grateful to Roberto Márquez and Ana Saldamando for sending me the text of this popular poem. The Spanish version is as follows:

> Cuatro esquinitas
> Tiene mi cama
> Cuatro angelitos
> Que me la guardan.
> Con Dios me acuesto,
> Con Dios me levanto,
> Con la Virgen María
> Y el Espíritu Santo.

100 Among the many examples of death imagery in Soriano's art see, for example, the 1957 *Skulls* (private collection,

Mexico), the 1978 *Skeleton with Flowers* (Fundación Cultural Televisa, Mexico), and the 1983 *Caged Death* (private collection, Mexico), reproduced in Museo Nacional, *Juan Soriano: Retrospectiva,* nos. 28, 40, and 44, respectively.

101 Malú Block, interview with the author, Mexico City, June 8, 2007.

102 Certain works by Soriano seem most akin to examples of Cadmus's painting. See, for example, *Point O'View* of 1945 (Williams College Museum of Art, Williamstown, MA) or *The Shower* of 1943 (private collection; illustrated in Lincoln Kirstein, *Paul Cadmus* [New York: Rizzoli, 1984], pp. 60, 62). Both were interested in old master technique applied to the depiction of quotidian subjects that often reflected homoerotic themes. Cadmus showed at the Midtown Galleries in New York in 1945, when Soriano was in Manhattan for the Knoedler show.

103 It should be stressed that the growing taste for abstract art in the United States in the 1940s was by no means all-pervasive, and realist painting (including Mexican) continued to appeal to many U.S. collectors with more conservative preferences.

Selected Bibliography

Principal Monographs

Briuolo Destéfano, Diana. *Juan Soriano: Pintor de antiguos y nuevos dilemas.* Mexico City: Consejo Nacional para la Cultura y las Artes, 1997.

Fernández, Justino, and Diego de Mesa. *Juan Soriano.* Mexico City: Universidad Nacional Autónoma de México, Dirección General de Publicaciones, 1976.

Fuentes, Carlos, and Teresa del Conde. *Juan Soriano y su obra.* Mexico City: Instituto Nacional de Bellas Artes, 1984.

Fundación Amparo, Puebla. *Celebración a Juan Soriano.* Puebla: Fundación Amparo, 2005.

González Esteva, Orlando. *Amigo enigma: Los dibujos de Juan Soriano.* Madrid: Ave de Paraíso Ediciones, 2000.

Grupo Azabache, Mexico City. *Juan Soriano: Los sueños moldeados.* Mexico City: Grupo Azabache, Consejo Nacional para la Cultura y las Artes, 2005.

Márquez, María Teresa. *Juan Soriano: Autorretrato.* Mexico City: Editorial Joaquín Mortiz, 1987.

Mutis, Alvaro, et al. *Juan Soriano, el poeta pintor.* Mexico City: Consejo Nacional para la Cultura y las Artes, 2000.

Paz, Octavio. *Juan Soriano: Retratos y visions.* Mexico City: Grupo Unido de Promoción y Asesoría, 1989.

Paz, Octavio, et al. *Juan Soriano: Retratos y esculturas.* Mexico City: Grupo Azabache, 1991.

Pitol, Sergio. *Juan Soriano: El perpetuo rebelde.* Mexico City: Consejo Nacional para la Cultura y las Artes, 1993.

Poniatowska, Elena. *Juan Soriano, niño de mil años.* Mexico City: Plaza y Janés, 1998.

Principal Exhibition Catalogues

Museo Amparo, Puebla. *Juan Soriano: La rebelión y la libertad.* Exh. cat. Puebla: Museo Amparo, 2005.

Museo de Arte Internacional Rufino Tamayo, Mexico City. *Juan Soriano: La creación como libertad. Homenaje nacional en su 80 aniversario.* Exh. cat. Mexico City: Museo de Arte Internacional Rufino Tamayo, 2000.

Museo de Arte Moderno, Mexico City. *Juan Soriano.* Exh. cat. Mexico City: Museo de Arte Moderno, 1978.

Museo Nacional Centro de Arte Reina Sofía, Madrid. *Juan Soriano: Aves de paso.* Exh. cat. Madrid: Museo Nacional Centro de Arte Reina Sofía, 2006.

Museo Nacional Centro de Arte Reina Sofía, Madrid. *Juan Soriano: Retrospectiva, 1937–1997.* Exh. cat. Madrid: Museo Nacional Centro de Arte Reina Sofía, 1997.

Museo Nacional de la Estampa, Mexico City. *Juan Soriano: Obra gráfica, 1944–2001.* Exh. cat. Mexico City: Consejo Nacional para la Cultura y las Artes, 2001.

Museo Soumaya, Mexico City. *Juan Soriano: Santo y seña.* Exh. cat. Mexico City: Museo Soumaya, 2006.

Index

Page numbers in italics indicate illustrations.